Qigong Master
Jim Nance

Published in 2024 by Guiding Qi, LLC

Disclaimer #1: This book is based on my personal recollections of events, recounted to the best of my knowledge and memory. Please note that to protect privacy, some identities have been changed or omitted. These alterations are meant to preserve the anonymity of the individuals involved. The details and dialogues have been reconstructed from memory and, while they reflect true events, they should be considered a representation rather than an exact historical account.

Disclaimer #2: The experiences and practices described in this book are based on the author's personal journey with qigong and do not represent the official curriculum or learning process of Spring Forest Qigong. The views expressed herein are solely those of the author and should not be taken as a substitute for professional advice from the Spring Forest Qigong organization. Those interested in pursuing Spring Forest Qigong's educational programs are encouraged to contact the organization directly.

Qigong Master Jim Nance

My Life Story Led Me Here

By Master Jim Nance and Naomi Joy Nance

When you think,

Think from the point of origination.

When you move,

Move from the place of regeneration.

When you feel,

Feel from the place of essence energy.

As you exist,

Exist from the place of emptiness,

And as you see,

Look for the Divine.

—Master Jim Nance

CONTENTS

Part I: On the Way

Part II: The Way

Acknowledgements

I am thankful for the help I receive daily on a spiritual level, from the divine, and from all the teachers and masters who came before. I want to thank Master Chunyi Lin, my teacher, my friend, for his ongoing support and guidance. My success in Qigong has been through him. Thanks to my wife Naomi for writing this book, my life story. There are so many people, some are named throughout these pages, many are not. I have had incredible support in this journey—thank you all. All the people I have worked with, all the healing—thank you for the opportunity, for the trust. Thank you to my brother Verge for being a constant voice of encouragement throughout my life. Thank you, family. I cannot say a big enough thank you to my father for helping me become who I became. And lastly, a person who is an inspiration to me—my daughter Anne. Thanks.

Jim Nance

About the Writing Process

The book wakes me in some dark hour of the early morning. It tells me: *get up, there is something waiting for you, and if you don't find a pen soon, it may fly by without being caught. You may never meet it again.*

So, I must get up in the dark and find my pen and paper. The image that comes to me first is of the two adolescent palm trees which hold residence in our backyard. Each, for the past several months, has hosted an imposing spear-like new leaf growth. From the center of the tree, they pierce into the blue sky with fierce uprightness. How does it not bend or break? And how does it know when is the right time to unfurl itself—becoming what it will become?

The stories of this book have unfurled to let me in over these past several years. For that, I am honored. The stories became alive as I listened to Master Nance share his life through conversation, classes, and lectures—and they became part of my life as well. One day, when the time was right, I sat down at my desk and started writing. The words flowed out like they had been waiting there all along.

And then the book began speaking to me—revealing its aliveness, its collaborative spirit. If I was missing some piece of information, for example, Jim would, without fail, usually through casual conversation, bring up the precise topic or story I was working on. I always listened with care, even if I did not think I had any question. That he was bringing up the same subject as I was working with, always, I knew, had some significance. I only had to wait, listen, and find out.

Other times, the book revealed direction to me through random sources—through images, or through something said in passing. Information that was needed or missing would inevitably appear. The relationship with this book has taught me a new way of writing. Now, when I write, the *listening* carries as much weight as the writing. There is a time to go, and a time to stop. Time to get up and walk away, or time to look out the window. And many times, the words flow and flow, and my fingers have had to race to catch the words before they launched out into the ether.

My goal in penning these stories has been to keep it simple, accessible, and to stay true to the spirit of Master Nance's voice, character, and teaching style. Of course, he has been here by my side all along (pretty much we have melded into one person by now). Our hope, in this collaborative project, is to present a book that many people, from many walks of life, can read—from young people, to elders, to people who have experience in Qigong, and those who never heard of it. This book, we believe, has something for everybody—and at variable depths.

There are two parts. First, the early life stories, pre-Qigong. The second section covers events which happened during the time Jim met Master Lin, and then worked with Qigong. Another difference you will see in the second part is the heavy use of *italics*.

The reason is this: during February 2023, we stayed in a cabin in northern Arizona to breathe the winter-desert air and work on the book. During this month, I asked Jim to speak on several specific topics, including healing, becoming a Master, and Qigong. I recorded these talks and transcribed them. The pieces of text in italics are from these transcriptions—they are pieces that needed to be left alone, largely un-edited. I found that the energy in the words was specific to the moment, and important to be as they were. Again, the book, the words, communicated with me throughout this entire process. If I edited something that was not supposed to be changed, I knew right away.

When the stories were ready, when they knew I was ready, they became what they were to become upon the page. More than a writer, I feel I am the assistant—one whose job it is to greet the guests, and to help them get settled. The guests are the words. I am here to open the door and help them find their spot on the page.

Naomi Joy Nance

Introduction Note

This is just what happened to me. I was so limited in my life—my parents didn't know if I could walk, or if I would ever talk. I was shuffled from place to place in a world full of fear and violence. I could not read. Through all that has unfolded in my life, I have truly seen a way out of no way. What I discovered in Qigong is an actualization of this. Everything is possible. I grew legs that could walk and run; I became an athlete. My mind healed and I learned to read—I became a teacher. From a boy who did not utter a word, to a person who could not only function and get by in the world, but one who could offer something in return—a way to help others, this is an example of a miracle. For a person like me to connect with someone like Chunyi Lin, an extraordinary Master from China— and to learn healing techniques that came through centuries of time—is an example of God at work. I have had the honor to be able to help many people through this healing art called Qigong; and continue to learn from others, from the great Masters of the past, who are helping still to this day. I am consistently stunned by the beauty and the gifts that have been part of this life.

When I look at my story from a distance, I see all the roads and paths, like lines on a map, leading me to where I am today. These stories came together with help from the divine, and I have been able to use them again and again to help others to see more clearly how this intelligent energy has been at work, all along, in their own lives. I encourage each of you, dear friends, to examine the map of your life. You will find there has been help; there has been beauty, gifts that came in many forms along the way.

Part I
On The Way

Soul Repair

That day, I sat silently and watched as Mr. Jenoc's hands worked the leather. They moved so fast I only saw them as a blur of motion. Once a week, my father sent me shuffling down the sidewalk toward the shoemaker's shop a couple of blocks over. The ritual always began with sweet ice on a stick—cherry or strawberry, not banana (that flavor didn't go well with the smell of tanning leather), and I sat there, among the stacks of shoes lining the walls, perched on the high-stool, and I watched his hands move.

"Son, if you can learn a trade," my father said, "you will always be alright."

To my father, learning a trade meant that you could offer something that was useful to people, something that was needed. In that way, he was certain, by knowing a skill or a trade, one would always be sure of finding a place in the world.

It was not my path to repair the soles of shoes, but to connect with my own soul and to help others to connect with theirs. This is my story—which includes a few adventures from my life—on my way to becoming a Qigong Master.

Junior is Alright

Coming into the world—there were some complications, to put it simply. I had a pale complexion. I was so pale that on my birth certificate they wrote "Caucasian," even though both of my parents had deep, brown-toned skin and were clearly African American. Next, the doctor said that something was wrong with my legs. They did not form right, particularly my feet, and that I would, in no way, be able to get around or walk, or function normally throughout my life. He informed my parents, and advised them it would probably be best to remove my legs from the knees down—immediately.

Fortunately, my parents did not heed this advice.

"My son's going to be alright," my father said.

I was named after my father: Sidney James Nance Jr.

Over the years, my parents, grandparents, aunts, uncles—anyone who oversaw my care—each day, twice per day, massaged my legs and feet. As they worked with my young limbs, they envisioned me as being healthy; running and playing with perfectly strong, perfectly formed legs and feet. They projected this image to me, to my spirit, as they worked—sending a powerful healing message through their love. Because of this dedicated care, I can walk today.

Soldier, Cowboy, Provider, Father

Iowa, mid-1900s: Cedar Rapids was a small, bustling, Midwest industrial town. Surrounded by corn and soy fields, several factories made their place in the center of the city. It was a blue-collar town; the factories attracting workers from around the country. A small percentage of African American families settled, many coming from the mines or from the south. They lived a lower to upper middle-class lifestyle, despite the ongoing racial tension. My father's family was a prominent part of this small middle class African American community. There is an ancient story of my great-great grandmother escaping slavery in the south. Carrying her baby in her arms, she walked all the way north and west to Iowa.

My father, Sidney James Nance, called Jim by most, rode bucking broncos, listened to country music in the morning over bacon and eggs; was a boxer, a soldier, and a friend. From doctors to hustlers, from Hollywood to the corner store, people from all walks of life would come to sit on our crooked old porch, examine the air, and trade words with my father. He was known across the land for his insight, his humor, and his generous spirit.

His laugh was otherworldly, and almost impossible to describe. Throwing his head back, it began with a high-pitched *eeee-eeeey!*

The note held for a spell, eventually transforming into a series of abrupt, chortling, staccato like sounds, before finally cascading into a round of unbridled nasal snorts. Anyone who heard him could not help but join in fits of laughter. It was contagious. The whole town knew of his laugh. Kids waved and giggled out the car windows as they passed by on the bustling street in front of our house.

For all his love of life, life dealt him a hard hand. At just twelve years old, he lost his father. After decades in the mines, the scars on his father's lungs left them too damaged to carry on. My father, the only son in the family, with four sisters and his mother, too soon became the man of the house and had to find a way to support them.

He found a place at the meat-packing plant. It spanned a half mile in all directions, dominating the small Iowa town. A heavy odor covered the neighborhoods, as thousands of cattle were crowded into corrals each day before being processed. My father, tall and muscular for his age, claimed to be older than he was (only twelve at the time), and was hired on. I will not go into detail about his work at the slaughterhouse—for good reason. He worked some of the worst positions imaginable, in places with names like "the hide cellar." It was here that his hands were transformed from many hours of pulling hides. One inch thick callouses covered each knuckle, and great pads covered his palms. His already big-for-his-age hands became terrifying to anyone who caught a glimpse. I noticed, in any photos of my father, or anytime I witnessed him in public, he kept his great hands hidden away, usually tucked behind his back.

There was just one time, I can recall, where he purposely exposed his calloused hands:

I was young, and he took me out to eat lunch at a restaurant. My father, whenever he went out, dressed exquisitely. He wore a tailored suit, quality leather shoes, a tie, and a hat. He dressed me handsomely that day too, and we took a cab downtown. When we got out of the cab, there was another man, a stranger, leaning up against the wall in the shadows of a nearby building. Right away, his eyes were on us. They were not friendly eyes. You must remember; this was the rural America of the mid-nineteen hundreds. Segregation and even lynching were not that far in the past. My father gave the stranger a polite nod. The man continued his dark, unmoving glare.

A sensitive kid, I could tell something was going on. Something was tense between the men, but I was too young to know what it all meant. My father paid the cabbie, and we were about to go into the restaurant, when instead, my father stood still. His gaze was fixed on the man, and the man was glaring back. And then my father made one subtle move—he brought his hands from behind his back and held them calmly, clasped together, in front of his body. I saw the man take one look at those giant hands, duck his head, and walk away.

All through junior high and high school, my father worked at the meat processing plant, going straight there after school every day, and working into the night. Somehow, he managed to do well academically, and proved talented as an athlete, including football, basketball, track, and boxing. Because of his high academic standing, and athletic merit, he was offered full scholarships to several big ten universities in the country, but due to his dedication to care for his mother and sisters, at least until they could find work on their own, he had to turn down his chance at higher education. More than a few times, I heard stories from people in the community about how my father helped them to get through school.

Our family dentist, always so kind, told me, after a thorough cleaning to my nine-year-old teeth, "If it wasn't for your father, I never would have passed my exams." He was beaming with gratitude.

Red Ball Express

After graduating, World War Two was in full swing, and my father was drafted. He fell into a unit labeled The Red Ball Express. Trucks loaded with highly flammable diesel fuel were to be delivered to the front lines—hence the name. All through the night, crossing dangerous, war-scarred land, the soldiers, many of whom were African American, drove trucks carrying their volatile loads. Some never made it to their destination. Later in the war, he found himself cleaning up after the horrors of concentration camps of Nazi Germany. He did not talk about the war—hardly ever. But what he wanted me to know was that he had given a great service to the nation.

There is one war story I wish to share—because it relates to my existence. My father told this story to me after I asked him the reason why he never drove a car.

Setting: somewhere in Europe.

One night, as the usual sounds of missile strikes growled through the air, surrounded by the engine roar of his big diesel, my father drove into the night. He had been driving for many hours. Too many. Eyes bleary, dust clouds from the wheels over torn roads playing tricks with shadows in the headlights, his head rocked with the heaviness of no rest and long days. My father, while behind the wheel, fell asleep. Suddenly, like a dream, like a nightmare—a man appeared in the road, directly in front of his unrelenting truck. In a brief flash of consciousness, waking with a jolt, he recognized this man. It was a friend—a gentle friend. And then stomping on the brakes with every inch of force in his body, the truck tore to a stop—gravel, dust, ravaged land flying. But it was too late. Like a dream, like a nightmare, this friend stepped out to stop the truck. This gentle friend—with only his body and the power of superhuman belief— stepped into the road to stop the truck before it launched over the edge of the cliff that would take my father's life, transforming the truck with its load into a fiery mass. This gentle young man, in his smallness, in his greatness, saved my father's life. For this, he gave his life. And because of this, I was able to come into the world. And because of this, my father never drove a vehicle again.

He wanted me to know this story; to know that there were people who gave a great deal for me to have a life—that my life was important, something of great value. He did not want me to forget this.

After the war, still a young man, my father took some time to travel west. His love for horses sent him to where he found work with ranchers and later rode bucking broncs in the rodeo. Touring with the rodeo, he made enough money—along with the occasional poisonous-snake-catching side jobs—to send home to his mother and sisters. After about a year of rambling, he returned to Iowa, and to life and work at the stockyard. His support for his family continued until his sisters were adults and could take care of themselves.

My father modeled the kind of person I needed to be to have the courage in life to do what I was going to do. He modeled kindness and compassion, strength, and caring for the people around him. When he came home from working all day at the factory, I often found him in the backyard, with a paper bag full of peanuts in hand, and squirrels surrounding him.

"Come on, son, you want to feed the squirrels?" He'd say, inviting me to join.

They waited around us like trained pets. Other days, he took his lariat out into the street, making a great lasso and showing off his cowboy rope tricks while the neighbor kids giggled and cheered with glee. And then, in the evening, in a crooked and dilapidated house, he relaxed in his armchair, stacks of books piled high on all sides. People, music, dancing, conversation, and hard work filled his days. With some, it seems clear—they are set on a path to love life as much as possible. It was this way with my father.

Dreamer, Teacher, Traveler, Mother

My mother's vision went far beyond the borders of a small Midwest town. For her children, she was determined, at every chance she got, to show them they need not limit themselves or their opportunities for the future. But this vision did not come easy.

My mother, Marion, was one of the most courageous people I have ever known. She faced violent trauma in her youth, and in such extremes that I believe most people in her position may not regain their right mind. Yet, she could rise above it and provide a beautiful life for her children.

Growing up in Iowa, her mother died when she was young, and her aunt (whom I knew as grandmother Naoma), raised her and a passel of other kids. Later, with three small children of her own, and hardly a dollar, my mother earned a college degree, proving to her children that there were possibilities beyond what we saw in our small-town community. Her creativity and grit carried her through and gave us an example to follow. She was constantly finding creative ways to point us toward the bigger world, toward broader options. She tried to involve us in as many learning opportunities as she could find. Every week, a woman came to our house to teach us German. We had lessons in gymnastics, swimming, baseball, and she made sure we learned to play musical instruments. Begrudgingly, I sat strapped to an accordion, while children outside the window laughed and played.

She taught us ways to look out for ourselves. Once, during a gymnastics class, my brother and were separated from the group. We were left with the equipment no one else wanted to use. While the other kids received the full attention from the teachers for the duration of the class, we were left on our own.

"They don't want to teach us anything. We just stood to the side while the other kids learned," my brother said when our mother asked about the class.

She was determined to find ways for us to explore, to thrive. But after hearing about gymnastics, she promptly took us out of the program. She wanted us to know that we did not need to be stuck where we were treated without respect. Throughout my time with her, I witnessed many examples of this lesson.

After she completed her degree and her kids were older, she traveled the world, living and teaching in several countries—Korea, Japan, Italy, Germany, Thailand, and on the continent of Africa—to name a few. Eventually, she ended up back in Iowa, teaching in the public school district. She became the first African American to attend the school and then to retire as a teacher in the same school.

Not long after my father and mother were married—sometime following World War Two, and before the factory workers' union—I came into the world.

In the Mood

Something was surely wrong, my mother thought. As a baby, I never cried or made any noise. I sat or laid in bed quietly as she went about her day. But she wasn't aware of what was really happening. I had the ability to move my consciousness out and away from my body. I could travel throughout the room and through the house at will, and could see any area I wished, all while still lying in the crib, not physically moving. As my mother went about her chores, doing laundry, making food, and meeting with family, I followed her invisibly—that is, my spirit-body followed her. She could not see me as I was with her, and only knew that I was content and quiet, lying in my bed all day. This is why I never felt the need to cry out—I always knew right where she was. Still, my silence caused her to worry.

My father also had concerns, but not about my abilities. His concerns were about the people who came to visit me. The combination of his experience with the atrocities of war and the grueling work at the packing plant caused my father to have high standards when it came to cleanliness and bacteria. Keeping a sanitary environment within our house was high priority. The news the doctor gave about my fragile condition at birth didn't help matters. So, anyone who came to visit, he insisted, must wear a mask over their nose and mouth while in my presence. I have early memories of masked faces looking down at me as I lay in the crib. Their eyes loomed above me, while mysterious muffled sounds came from behind the cloth covering their faces.

One afternoon, some family members were over, chatting and being social in the living room, when my uncle heard something coming from my room. He decided to spy on me, listening with his ear pressed against the door. After a few moments, he went running back to the group.

"You've got to check this out. The little guy is saying something!"

Never had I made a sound up to this point, but there I was, sitting alone in the dark of my room, while a surprised, masked audience listened outside.

"I'm in the mood... for love." Softly, with a somewhat gravelly, unsteady, one-and-a-half-year-old voice—I crooned these first words.

Little did I know that in just two weeks, my life would transform completely.

Divided and Invisible

Around this time, in the mid-1900s, workers' unions were forming across the country. The packing plant where my father worked was also forming a union—except African American workers were not permitted to join. After what my father had been through in the war—the sacrifice he made, risking his life—he decided it was not fair to be blocked from the union. He made his mind up that he was going to fight for his right, and for others, to be a part of it.

The community respected my father in a big way. He was always doing things to help others. Several times, he helped new businesses get started, and as a result; he had made many connections and friends. So, when he stood up to be acknowledged by the union, it was a big deal in our small town. He had been working at the stockyard since he was twelve years old. The people at the factory were like a second family. Also, there were other African Americans, as well as women, and immigrants working there; they too faced denial from the union. All these people, plus people in the community and town, were behind him, supporting him in joining. When the time came to request admission formally, people of all kinds, many workers—black, brown, white, men, and women—a whole crowd accompanied him.

At the same time, there was another group—one who fiercely opposed his direction. They wanted things to stay the way they were. They were afraid of changes. Every so often, a group of angry men would show up outside of our house, demanding that my father come out to confront them, to face them and fight. As each day grew dark and as evening approached, the tension grew as my mother and father anticipated violence and prepared for the inevitable.

My parents concluded it would be the worst thing if I, as a young child, had to witness my father getting hurt, or possibly even losing his life. With heavy hearts, they made the decision that I should go away to live with my aunt on the other side of town.

The separation from my parents shattered my world. I was a silent child normally, content to be by myself for hours. But that day, as a stranger carried me away, I watched as the form of my mother faded into the distance, and for the very first time in my life—I cried, and I cried.

Later, while lying in a small room at my aunt's house, sobbing into exhaustion, suddenly, a little girl appeared next to me. She was sitting on the bed, softly brushing the top of my head with her hand. In a lulling, small voice, she assured me it was going to be ok. I looked up at her, a feeling of warm comfort washed over me. She had straight, light blonde hair, and was only a couple of years older. I don't know how she got there, but there she was—kind and gentle, soothing me with her soft voice. I noticed there was someone else in the room. The narrow silhouette of a woman stood silently in the shadows against the far wall. She had stark white hair, and even though the room was dark as night, it seemed there was a faint light glowing around her. I would encounter both mysterious people again, only many years later.

Two long years went by at my aunt's house. Like a ghost, I floated in and out of doorways, rarely speaking, silently observing the faces and sounds of my environment, then fading away again. If I learned my mother was going to visit, I made sure to disappear. My hurt was deep, and I could not let myself see her face. I felt perpetually disconnected from the world around me. It was here at my aunt's house, to everyone's amazement (because of the complications with my feet), that I learned to walk. In a photograph, I see myself on my feet at age two or three, with arms outstretched, crying, and reaching toward my father—my first steps.

One day, while playing alone in my room at my aunt's, I said to myself: *I wonder if I can disappear.* Then, I walked to the mirror. *I was gone!* There was no image of me looking back from the mirror. A little surprised, I ran back to the other side of the room. Then, with slower steps, I returned to look in the mirror. *I was back!*

"Auntie, Auntie!" I called out. "I can disappear!"

"Ok, Jimmy," my aunt said with a slight chuckle, not looking up from folding clothes. "Let's see what you can do."

I ran out into the living room, where she sat with the laundry.

"Look, look!" I said. "I'm disappeared!"

Then I saw my aunt's face transform into a look of absolute fear. Her smile dropped, the skin around her mouth grew stiff, and her eyes darted around the room.

"Jimmy," she said in a quiet but tense tone, "I want you to come back now. Ok...come on back."

So, I ran back into the bedroom (where I reappeared), and then returned to the living room.

My aunt beckoned me to come near to her. In a serious tone, more serious than I had ever heard from her, she said, "Jimmy, never, ever, ever do that again. You understand? If you ever do this, someone will come and take you away."

"Ok Auntie, I will never do it again." I said.

And I stayed true to my word. I never became invisible again.

The Party

On the other side of town, my father continued his struggle for inclusion in the union. After two years, they finally granted him membership. The tension and the violent threats eventually subsided, and I could return home.

Soon after the reunion with my family, was my fifth birthday. Something moved me that day. Without my parents' knowledge, I wandered the neighborhood, going from door to door.

Knocking on the front door, and waiting for someone to appear, I said: "Hello, my name is Jim Nance. I moved back home with my mom and dad, and I would like to invite you to my birthday party tomorrow. Please come. There will be cake and ice cream."

I covered the blocks surrounding our house, inviting as many people as I could. I walked about four blocks—a lot of ground for a 5-year-old. The next day, the day of my birthday, my father sat on the front porch. A cake and a small bucket of ice cream sat on the table inside. First, only a couple of people showed up, then another group of about three or four walked into the house, and then another, and another. My parents gave each other a long look from across the room. They were a little bewildered. *Why were all these strangers, people they hadn't invited, coming to the house?* But they graciously went along with it, smiling, welcoming them in. After speaking to a few of the guests, they found out about my neighborhood venture—their shy son, who hardly spoke a word, had invited them all.

In no time, the backyard was so full of people, my father had to run out for more cake and ice cream. I became overwhelmed by the crowd and climbed high into the big maple tree to get some space. I sat on a branch looking down on the whole thing. Eventually, there was some restless stirring below. People had noticed I was missing. It was my father who spotted me up in the old tree and waved me to come down. As I made my descent, everyone sang the Happy Birthday song. Huge tears rolled down my face, not because I was afraid, not because I was sad, but because I knew that never again would a birthday be as great as that one.

Play Ball

They wore silk or velvet suits, felt or straw hats. Some had shiny leather shoes, others wore suede. To me, they were almost unreal, like super-humans. Never had I seen men who dressed so splendidly—

and they were African American, like me. Not only were their suits tailor made to fit in the finest way, but they modeled perfect sculptures of athleticism—every muscle and tendon so defined, they seemed poised to leap off the skeleton individually. These men were members of the famed Negro Baseball League.

During his westward travels after the war, my father, with his keen athletic skill, formed friendships with some of these men. Although he was never officially part of the League, every year, a group of guys came to our raggedy house in Cedar Rapids to visit to play baseball. Since African Americans weren't allowed in professional baseball at a national level, they formed the League. Organized tournaments started, and men from all over the country—some of the most incredible athletes—played in these games. I was in awe when I saw them show up at our house. I hovered in the doorway, watching them laugh and joke around with my father. I had never seen such men. In their mannerisms, they showed such confidence, such poise. They made a marked impression on my young mind.

We all went to the baseball field that day. I had never, until that time, witnessed my father engage in sports, and I was never to see it again. It was to be the first and last time. Although he never spoke of it, throughout high school, my father played sports, and he was talented. As I sat in the stands that day with my mother, I held my breath as my father stepped up to the plate.

CRACK!—I heard the ball as it met the wooden bat. I saw my father's crouched figure as he sprang to run. But then—I saw nothing. He was so fast; he disappeared into the air. One moment he was there, the next, amidst a dust-filled cloud, he was at first base. But the most extraordinary thing was what I felt as he ran. The sound and vibration that traveled through the earth, and then up through the bleachers where I sat, and then up through my own legs—as his feet pounded against the ground—is something I will never forget. It was magical. The ground beneath where we sat quaked and boomed with his every step. He became an earth moving giant—to me, the physical embodiment of thunder.

The other shock came immediately after he hit the ball. The crowd around me reacted in unison. An enormous collective *hiss* rose up like a wave as everyone in the stands inhaled at once. For a moment, every breath was suspended, and the world paused in a sharp silence—and then a roaring, whooshing sound poured out from the crowd, like a great surge of air and heat and noise releasing from its locked chamber. The experience moved me to the core. It was then and there I firmly decided what I was going to be. I would become a professional athlete.

Grandmother

In the summer, my uncles often threw the football around my grandmother's yard, tackling one another to the ground. They were big and rough. At eight years old, I longed to join them, but my grandmother wouldn't allow it. She knew I'd get hurt. Sometimes, when I thought she wasn't looking, I'd sneak out and run onto the playing field.

My grandmother's name was Naomi. We called her Naoma—but with a short "o," so it came out sounding more like Nelma. It is said that grandmother came from an indigenous tribe, though she never wanted to talk about it. At a young age, authorities forcibly removed her from her family and enrolled her in a federal boarding school. Later, she married my grandfather, had many children, and made the best cakes and pies in the county.

When she was a young girl, she could walk on her hands all the way to school (about ten blocks); and stories tell that while in elementary school, she ran a race against the renowned Olympiad, Jesse Owens. I can picture it—two dark slim kids lined up along a pocked dirt road on a balmy southern summer day, my grandmother barefoot, her skirt hiked up. They took off in a flash, kids yelling and cheering along the sidelines, a slight trail of dust, like smoke, followed in their wake; brown feet sailing over the worn dirt road like spirits in flight. They say she won the race that day against Owens. And, knowing her, I believe it to be true. Even in her later years, she was exceedingly strong.

One lazy spring day, while I was sitting around her house with the family, my grandmother's voice broke the silence, "Well, who wants to play catch with me?"

First, I was a little shocked to hear her say that. I had never known my grandmother to play catch, or any game at all. And then I watched in astonishment as all around the room, my uncles and aunts seemed to slink down into their chairs, their eyes averted, looking at the ground, as if there were answers written between the floorboards. Some of them got up and walked solemnly and swiftly from the room without a word. I was confused. My aunts and uncles were strong and hard-headed—two of them were championship boxers. *Why this act?* It was as if they were afraid of my grandmother. The moment of silence left an eerie tension in the room.

"I'll play!" I said, jumping up from my chair and breaking the stiff quietude. My uncle shot me a sideways good-luck-you're-going-to-need-it look as he left the room.

So, I got the ball and gloves and lined up on the street, my grandmother at the other end. I readied myself to catch the ball. Barely had I set my feet in place on the pavement, barely had I looked up when—WHAM!—the ball hit my glove so hard, my hand didn't start stinging until a couple of seconds after. Amazed at how precise her aim was—I didn't need to change position or move my glove hand—only held it up, and the ball hit the center perfectly. I stood there stunned, staring down the street where my grandmother's slight frame marked the distance.

"Ok, now throw it back," she hollered.

I lobbed it back to her and—ZING! Again, she threw the ball so fast, and so precise, I had no time to see it coming, and yet there it was, in the heart of my glove. Soon, my gloved hand felt as if it was burning up. Well, this kept up for a while. I cannot describe the mixture of wonder and fear that came to me over the mystery of my grandmother; yet I was determined not to quit.

It took me many years to understand my grandmother's lesson.

She saw from watching me play football with the older boys that I lacked a healthy amount of fear. I lacked the understanding of fear that I needed in order to be safe. So, in her own wild and loving way, she showed me that there were things bigger and stronger than myself. I needed to have a concept of my own limitations and to experience the possibility that I could get hurt. So, without really hurting me, and with love, she taught me this lesson.

I knew there was something special about my grandmother the day I first heard her speak to me without talking. I was in a room full of people, including my aunts and uncles. Often, as a boy, I sat alone, observing but not taking part, as the group moved and swayed all around me. When I was young, I had no internal dialog. No thoughts busied my mind. I only observed, always within the present. My mother, and perhaps others, suspected something was wrong—something off balance because I didn't engage with others often, or talk much at all. My grandmother, though, seemed to know and understand me at a different level. I always felt her support, her protection, and her love for me. I was watching as my grandmother welcomed an important guest. He was a world championship boxer, and quite famous. His name was Joe Lewis, and he was interested in my uncle. He wanted to play a role in his future career in boxing. There was a buzz and excitement in the air—it was a big deal. I noticed that there was so much love and a lot of pride coming from my grandmother and the other family members. They were happy and proud to be who they were. They were proud of my uncle's accomplishments. I could feel the continuity of support throughout the room. It was then; I heard a unique voice in my head. It was distinctly her voice—my grandmother's.

She said, "This is what it's like to be a family. This is what we do for each other. This is how we show love and care for one another."

At first, I was confused. I looked all around the room. *Didn't anyone else hear what I heard?* Everyone was going about their business, chatting, moving about like no one said a thing. I looked over at her, and she looked at me and smiled, her eyes twinkling and shining. She knew I heard her. She said it again, directly to my mind, and her lips did not move. Throughout the years, she continued to speak to me in this special way.

Jumping Words

I tried to follow the words on the pages of my school textbook, but they jumped around. They moved from place to place like nervous ants, and I could not track them. I could not seem to make them keep still to see what they said. Sometimes, the entire sentence would slither away, each word like an alive thing, sliding off the page. Or half of the page would fade away, only to reappear in another section. Words were popping in and out of the page, disappearing, and playing visual tricks for as long as I looked at the book. A similar thing happened with sound. I would hear a person say something, but the words could switch places, or the consonants change positions to form completely new words.

I looked around the room, observing the other children as they read. It seemed they could look at the page and follow the lines like it was very simple. I watched as they traced the words across the page with their finger, their lips formed the words as they read. They understood the information coming from the page. *Why couldn't I?*

This was how it was for me, and still is at times. I was experiencing severe auditory and visual dyslexia. When I was a child, though, dyslexia was not a well-known disorder. School was something I would have excelled at, but instead, it became a place of constant fear and anxiety. I was excellent at math. The equations and numbers didn't jump around like words. I was one of the top students in math during elementary school, but once the teacher introduced word equations, I could not keep up, and fell behind. I told no one about what was happening, not my parents, nor my brother. It was a constant source of humiliation for me, and I lived in fear and worry of being found out. Both of my parents excelled academically, and many family members had college degrees, which was significant for African Americans in those days. My older brother seemed to fly through his classwork like it was nothing.

The pressure for me to do well in school felt immense, and I felt I could not meet it, not even part way. I hid my frustration and inability to read with an artful avoidance. I became a master at hiding my inability. This, I decided, was another reason I needed to be more-than-good at sports. I needed to be excellent. I saw that, because of my challenges with learning and reading, my future could not depend on the conventional means of going through school and landing a career. Becoming a successful athlete, I believed, was the only chance I had to make it in the world; to live a normal life, to have a family, to have stability.

Even though I convinced myself that no one knew I couldn't read, looking back, I am sure that both of my parents knew. One way they showed their love and protection toward me was to never bring this topic forward. They never asked me to read. They never wanted me to look into their eyes and see them looking at me in a humiliated state. Somehow, through a combination of divine intervention, help from other students, and my talent as an athlete, I made it through primary school and graduated.

The Run

Before each child was born, my mother had a dream. And the dream would foretell her child's future direction in life. She dreamt my older brother would be a man of business, my younger brother in entertainment, and I would be a "holy man." Later in my life, after traveling and meeting with medicine people and indigenous people, I realized that the way my mother had of dreaming her children was very much like what I encountered in Africa.

Because I did not speak until I was older, my mother was worried. *How can my son be a holy man if he cannot speak?* And then again, later, when I became absorbed in sports and pursuing the life of an athlete, she worried. *How can my son be a holy man if he is an athlete?* She did everything she could to discourage me from sports. But sports and I were destined to be. My relationship with my physical self and my athletic ability proved to play a vital role in my life—from education, to service, to spirituality. In my life, with what seemed like many limitations, being an athlete, I decided, was the surest and possibly the only path for me to move forward into a future. So, I went for it with everything I had.

One early morning, when I was eight years old, I awoke with a firm idea in mind—I was going to run. I decided that from the time the door opened to the community center, to the time they locked that same door—I would run on the track. So, that morning, I was there waiting as someone showed up to unlock the door at 8 am. I had never seen the man before. Usually, there was someone else managing the center, but today he happened to be there. He was filling in. I told him my plan to run. He didn't say much, and he didn't stop me. He just opened the door. I went to the track, and I ran and ran... and I ran. As the sun went across the sky, I ran. In the afternoon, my older brother Verge appeared and jogged along with me for a minute.

"What are you doing?" he asked.

"I'm running." I told him.

"How long are going to run?" He asked me.

"Until it's closed," I said.

"But that's 8 hours!" He exclaimed.

And after a pause, still jogging along beside me, he said, "You know—you are no ordinary person!"

Then he left.

Something within me that day led me onto that track. By exerting my body so intensely, something was shifting inside. Something that needed to change. The extreme level of physicality was moving me to a new place. A place where I could find myself. The ground beneath my bones vibrated with every step—the running rhythm, the essence of life, pounded through my body—calling out to my spirit, beckoning for union.

Hours later, the man in charge packed things up for the day, stacking the chairs, and sweeping the floor. Soon it was 4 pm.

He walked to the door of the community center, turned around and called out to me on the track, "Ok, that's it."

I ran up, and he locked the door behind me. I had been running for eight hours without pause.

"What's your name, son?" The coach asked.

"Jim Nance," I told him.

He would not forget my name, nor what he witnessed that day. Little did I know then that this man would play a significant role in my future, and I in his.

Leaving

"God will make a way out of no way," my mother said as she packed our bags.

After the divorce, my mother received full custody of us kids. For three years, the courts allowed me to see my father for only two hours each weekend. Once again, I found myself separated from him. The grief was a churning chaos within me, threatening to grow into a dark storm. I became a kid always on edge with no way to understand my emotions, and nowhere to place them. Fights became a frequent occurrence at school. Sports helped me, only somewhat, to let go with some of my excess energy and anger, and my older brother Verge was a constant force of support to me. All throughout my time as a kid, he was one person I could rely on to be there, to have my back. A true, generous spirit, he was (and still is) always cheering me on—always happy to celebrate in my successes.

My mother planned to live in Yellow Springs, Ohio, to go back to school and become a nurse. The other reason she wanted us to live in this area was for the unique experience it offered her sons. My older brother was showing signs of despair, like he didn't believe he had much in the way of a future. Though there were many amazing people in the community where we lived in Iowa—hard workers, dedicated family people, and some with advanced degrees—options seemed fairly limited for a young man coming into the world. Several of my brother's friends were getting into trouble, getting arrested, and some were dropping out of school. It was mainly a working-class lifestyle there, because of the many factories and industrial plants in the city. Even though my mother had a decent house and a steady job, she believed we needed to leave. What she saw happening with her oldest son did not paint a picture of the life she imagined for us. Following her intuition, she made a move to get away from the mid-west town where I was born.

We left with only a few things and just enough money to buy one bag of peanuts each. I was not happy to leave Iowa, because it meant leaving my father. Nothing made sense to me. The world seemed unfriendly. Strangers at every stop eyed us suspiciously. I was on guard constantly. Over the two-day bus ride, I fell into a dark mood, believing it was a mistake for us to leave. Finally, the bus pulled into a small town, where rolling green hills dotted with cows, horses, and sprawling oaks greeted us. We shuffled out in Yellow Springs, Ohio: a woman with three young boys—hungry, no money, no idea where to stay—but *God will make a way out of no way.*

The Woods

We moved into a mysterious woodland community on the outskirts of Yellow Springs. The land was like a place where dwarves or elves might live. Pathways crisscrossed through golden-leafed aspen, their tops shimmering in the sunlight. In my young life, I had little opportunity, so far, to spend time in the forest. Everything there was foreign, mysterious, and magical. After leaving Iowa and being separated once again from my father, the woodlands and nature of our new surroundings would prove to be like a soothing balm, a medicine—helping to heal my aching heart. For the first time, I could feel the aliveness of the earth beneath my feet, and myself part of it.

There were only a couple dozen people living in the forest glen: professors, writers, people from distant lands, and artists. My mother, my two brothers, and I moved into the converted attic of an old farmhouse. The air was thick with life. Noises of insects, rustling leaves, and the smell of wood smoke and coffee would carry us each morning as we walked the long dirt road to where the school bus arrived to pick us up.

Several strange and incredible homes dotted the land. I went inside a house that, from the outside, looked like an enormous pile of rusted metal mixed with bits of glass. On the shady side of the pile, a huge wooden door hid beneath the leafy branches of a tree. It opened to a great stairway that led down into an underground space. I looked up from the bottom floor of the house to see flecks of light coming through small glass openings in the walls and ceiling, sending colorful sparks dancing around the perimeter. The house transformed into an otherworldly cavern, glittering with light.

Another dwelling appeared, at first, as a shack made of nearly rotten wood—something you might come across while out hiking, and after one look, you might easily dismiss it as a long-abandoned house, nothing worth putting a lot of time into. But upon closer inspection, by standing still, letting the forest breeze move around you, you might notice—hidden expertly within the cracks and crevices of the knobby wood—a finely crafted doorknob. Inside, the dwelling was spacious and beautiful. Wide, hand-hewn columns supported the ceiling, and custom woodwork framed the space with masterful precision. The land entranced me. All was alive. There was more green abundance in the world around me than I thought possible. I was in a state of wonder all the time.

Within a great mound of dirt and moss, which was a house, lived a Japanese Zen nun. She invited my mother to a traditional tea ceremony. My mother decided it was an opportunity for me to have a cultural experience, so I went along. I was about twelve years old. Before we arrived, she instructed me—I would need to have patience and be quiet. We were about to witness a very special ceremony. She was always making efforts to expose her kids (especially me, since she believed it was my destiny to follow a religious path) to different spiritual orientations.

The nun moved around the room slowly, silently—cleaning the bowls, wrapping them in thin cloth, pouring steaming water from one container into another. I had never seen a woman with no hair before. I watched and listened to the gentle sounds of water bubbling, water being poured, the soft clicking sound of utensils being set upon a surface. Her feet padded across the dirt floor, soft as cat's feet, and the sound of breath—my own, in and out, inhale, exhale. The forest was breathing with me. The dirt hut was breathing with the forest.

I felt a sensation in the room as this was happening. Something I had never felt before. I did not know what it was, but I was aware that there was something very unusual about this woman and what she was doing. Usually, as I observed, a lot of questions would go through my head, a constant internal dialogue—*Why is this? What is that? What does it mean?*

But here in the dirt house, during the tea ceremony, I found myself doing something different. Instead of asking questions, it was then that I decided to start listening. I wanted to listen and be moved into life. I saw and felt an energetic presence as I listened in stillness. The ceremony seemed to go on forever, and I was lulled, like a daydream, into the rhythm of it—and then I went beyond it. When it was over, I was a different person. As I left the Zen nun's mound of dirt—the trees were different, my walk was different, the air was different.

The Two Little Girls

Because I was a boy of few words, my mother did what she could to encourage me to have conversations. One day, she brought me over to an unfamiliar house. She told me I was to go upstairs and into the room at the end of the hall. In that room, I would find two little girls.

"Just talk to them for fifteen minutes. These girls are very special," was all she said.

For the whole of these girls' lives (they were about seven and eight-years-old), they had been living in a severely confined and dark space, with almost no contact with the outside world. They spent every day locked inside of a small closet. Someone had cared for their basic needs, like food and water, but they never left the darkness of the closet. Having spent little time around other humans, besides one another, they did not speak and knew nothing about common social behavior. The adults who were in control in this situation believed it would be good for them to be with a child closer to their own age, and my mother thought it would also be good for me to practice talking. But my mother also knew something else. She had a premonition that there was something special in me that may help to connect to these two girls.

So, up the stairs I climbed, one foot in front of the other, not feeling eager at all to meet with this mysterious situation, and of course, not all that excited about having to talk. Approaching the room at the end of the hall, I noticed a faint light coming from beneath the doorway. The crack of light widened as I opened the door.

There, I saw three chairs; two were occupied. As I moved into the empty seat, the two little girls sat across from me—unmoving, unblinking, eyes wide—staring. I don't know if you remember being twelve years old, but as I recall, fifteen minutes at that age is a long time. And combined with the fact that I rarely spoke to anyone for any number of minutes, made this a challenging task. I didn't know what to do.

After a moment of awkward staring and silence between us, I started talking. And I did not stop. Anything that came to mind, came out in words—my brother, the sidewalk, the neighbor, the old barn down the block where we played, anything to make the minutes go by. I rambled on and on. Never had I been able to talk when no one was talking back. Also, it was a rarity to have no adults around to say what was right or wrong. I just talked and talked, like it was easy. All the while, the girls sat still as stone—statuesque and odd. This ritual went on every week. Up the stairs, I would go to the room with three chairs.

One day, though, as I approached the familiar stairway, I knew something was different. I could feel it, but I didn't know what it was. As I approached the door to the room at the end of the hall, the feeling became stronger. As I reached for the worn-out doorknob—its ceramic coat faded away in the center, dim light reflecting off the exposed brass—I felt a strange buzzing sensation. It was all around me, in the air, like electricity. I sat down in my chair, like usual, and started my ritual chatter. I felt as though I were watching myself. My mouth moved, the words came, yet I was unattached. I watched myself and I watched the room as if from a distance. But all the time, the buzzing feeling was still there, growing thick; and it was hard to ignore.

And then I made some dramatic gesture. I made a screwed-up face and pitched myself from the chair. When I looked over at the little girls, they had transformed. A wide grin had spread across each of their usually blank faces. For the first time, these two human beings sat in front of me, beaming with smiles.

It was as if they did not really know what was happening to their faces—as if those muscles relegated to smiling were never exercised before—like new muscles were learning an awkward new form. They glanced at each other, and then at me, and just kept grinning. I was so astonished that I leapt up from my chair and dashed from the room, calling out to my mother.

"Mother! Mother!… something's happening!" I was hysterical.

"Get back up there and keep doing whatever you're doing!" She shooed me away.

I knew that what happened in the room that day had something to do with the extraordinary buzzing feeling that came to me. I would never forget that feeling, that energy. Something mysterious happened that allowed communication between me and the girls—an understanding on a deeper level, one that initiated the beginning of healing for them. This was one of the earliest experiences that I was aware of in which I experienced energy as a helpful and intelligent force. Somehow, I knew it helped me; and it helped vitality to reach out to these girls. They had been through a highly traumatic experience. The people around them had tried their best to help, but still could not get through. Yet, someone like me—a young boy who wore funny shoes, who was shy and couldn't read—I could get through to them.

Just as the girls, with a smile, came into themselves, I too came into myself, and into a new world. My perception of myself and my ability had elevated. I knew then that I had something special, something to offer; a way I could help others. It was then that my life's purpose reached out to me and said—*Here you are, and you can do something special, something helpful.*

I used this experience time and time again throughout my life as I worked with children, some of whom were involved in deeply troubling experiences—and especially then. This same feeling that I discovered with the two little girls—the buzzing, electric sensation—would awaken in and around me. No matter what the situation, no matter what the challenge, I found a way to communicate, to get through to the children, and always in a way that was best for them. I was called upon to step in with many kids throughout my life, kids that no one else could find a way with. Without fail, when I felt that energetic feeling approach, a great calm entered the situation, and I knew everything would be alright. We were able, together, from that point, to reach a higher understanding, a healing place. What a gift.

Growing Pains and the Matinee

One morning, only a couple of weeks after the healing experience with the little girls, I awoke with an intense sensation all over my body. It felt as if my skin was on fire. Drifting in and out of consciousness, I battled with an incredible fever that lasted for days. The doctors came and went. My mother was worried, but no one had any answers or diagnosis. They kept me inside the house and out of sight.

Eventually, the fever broke. When I was strong enough to walk, I got out of bed and went to the mirror. What I saw was terrifying. My skin was coming off. Gauzy, translucent sheets peeled away in layers. The surface of my entire body transformed. Patch by patch, I shed my skin. Underneath, as if scorched by the sun, I was bright pink—and raw. I was like a new baby just coming into the world. The air, the breeze, even the light, felt as abrasive as sand. Many weeks passed by until I could go outside again.

When great changes happen to us in our lives, often they are given a name or a title, and then we accept them and move on. As babies, we experience colic, as toddlers, tantrums and teething, but some changes are mysterious—they have no name. What I experienced with my shedding, peeling skin had no name. Doctors, parents, no one seemed to know anything about the cause.

Later, I spoke of this situation to a shaman, a medicine man, and he told me that if I had been born at a different time, perhaps in a different culture—what I experienced would have significance, perhaps a sign of special abilities. In his culture, he said, they would train me in the way of a medicine person.

My body continued changing and transforming rapidly. I started growing at an alarming rate. At times, I was in such pain, I rolled back and forth in my bed howling and moaning all night long. At school, it was excruciating to do anything. To sit still for any length of time was torture. Getting up from a seated position sent sharp jabbing pains through my legs, and as we all know, school involves a lot of sitting. I walked around like I was two-hundred-years-old, stooped, and dragging my feet, and by the time I was into my twelfth year, I had reached the height of six foot two inches.

One day, I went to the movie theater with some friends to see a matinee. We were all around the same age, and that day the theater was offering a special price for kids twelve and under. When it was my turn to buy a ticket at the box office, they refused to sell it to me at the discounted rate. I was so tall, they did not believe I was only twelve years old. To my dismay, while my friends scuttled inside to take their seats for the show, I had to call my mother—her infuriation overshadowed my humiliation at the situation.

She marched into the theater with my birth certificate. After that, I never tried to get in to see a movie on the kid discount again. On the other hand, due to my unusually tall size, I could go through the door with no problem to see all the adult movies I wanted.

The Horse

A heavy sadness clung to me on that day. It came in like a great wave, and swelled all around me, pressing me toward the ground. It was hard to be separated from my father. On this particular day, I was with a group of boys, and they wanted to take me to see the horses. Walking along the dirt road, we came to an open, green field. A few horses grazed in the distance. After climbing under the fence, we sat in the grass to watch them. The day was still, bright and warm. A large dappled grey horse separated from the herd and came towards us. As he came closer, it was clear he was coming directly to me. I sat still as he inspected me with his enormous nostrils. Breathing gusts of hot, sweet-smelling air at my face with each exhale, the horse towered above me. Then he adjusted his position, so that the long side of his back was directly in front of me.

"This horse likes you," a boy said.

"He wants you to ride," another boy said.

And before I knew what was happening, I was sitting on the back of this massive horse. There was no saddle. As the horse started out, I gripped tightly onto its mane. We trotted off. I was bouncing all around the horse's back, and just when I was thinking, *goodness, this is so uncomfortable... this can't be right* (I had seen many western movies, and those cowboys did not bounce all over on top of the horse), we approached the edge of the pasture. The horse slowed down, and I breathed a sigh of relief. But then he turned to face the length of the field, gave one great snort, nodded his powerful head, and took off into a full gallop. *Yeee!* The ground rushed by in a blur. I was riding the wind. How smooth and how natural it felt on top of the horse. As he ran, he made subtle adjustments, consistently using the muscles in his back to help keep me centered. I could feel, and I knew, that he was always aware of me, always taking care to help me stay on.

We raced all the way down the field, and circled back to where my friends waited. He gently came to a stop there, and I slid off, collapsing to the ground, huge tear drops rolling down my face. It was not out of surprise or fear that I wept, but for the beauty of what I had just experienced—and for my father. My father was a horse person. Even though I always felt the presence of my father's love—no matter where I was—I felt wounded by his absence. This horse helped to heal my heart. To let me know I was never alone. There was always love available to me; there was care. Over the course of a year, I went often to visit this horse. We galloped through the pasture and remained friends for a long time.

My experience at this community surrounded by woods and field, offered me the opportunity to find my place in the world and to find solid ground. Before this time, throughout my life, I felt like I was spinning. When trauma occurs in a child's life, they can lose a sense of connection with themselves. A loss of safety, of continuity, can do this. Nothing felt real to me in the world—and then I found anger. This extreme emotion was something, even if only for a short period, that enabled me to feel a reconnection to myself. I had become distanced from my body and the life around me. I disassociated, living a dream-like existence.

When, as a young child, just as I was able to form my first words, I was taken away from my family— from the only safe-haven I knew—the stability I needed to mature emotionally was severed. From then on, I was living in a haze, and didn't have the tools to realize it. A thick fog covered my world. As a result, as a boy, I did bizarre things to bring myself back—like tackle trees, or jump off great heights, or run for hours. I was constantly trying to shake myself out of the oppressive fog I felt entrenched in. When I had to be separated from my father again at age twelve, things got worse. In part, this informed my mother's decision to move to another town. She had an innate sense of things. For the sake of her children, for the sake of their future, she knew she needed to initiate a drastic change.

Discovering that relationships were possible with beings other than humans—like with the horse, the woods, the earth—opened a door for me. Something hard within me began slowly to melt away and soften. The horse chose me that day. The shift that happened within me was not a result of something jarring or violent, but the opposite—I was changing because of caring, loving action. It was an experience of transformation. I could feel the life force in things—the leaves, the soil, and rocks, and I realized I was never separated from anything. I knew this presence, this intelligence, would be there for me for the rest of my life. Being in nature helped me to return to myself, though I had a long way to go. A pattern of seeking extreme experiences had made its place within me. This would be a pattern in my life, through many more years to come, and a passion that would prove hard to break—like full-contact sports.

Into the Game

Even though my mother wanted to keep me far from the world of sports, she recognized I had a serious need to release physical energy. I was getting into fights at school, and she could see that it would help to have somewhere else to focus my energy, somewhere that wouldn't get me into trouble. So, finally, she allowed me to try out for football. There was no team at the local school, so I had to enroll at a school the next town over, and hitchhike or find a ride each day. To me, this was hardly an obstacle if it meant I could play the sport I felt I was destined to play.

Everyone on the team buzzed with excitement at the prospect of playing professional football—and this was also what I wanted. I played with such fervor and energy, when I hit and tackled other players, I hit hard—too hard. The helmets, back then, were of such poor quality that the consistent impact to my head was beginning to have repercussions. Eventually, when I ran into another player and jarred my head—I went temporarily blind. Everything turned completely white—bright white light, and that was all. One time, my vision did not return to normal for several hours. I didn't want anyone to know. I loved the game, and more than that, I believed it was my future. Determined, at all costs, to hold on to that vision of myself, I was willing to put myself at risk of serious injury. Once, after a collision when I lost my sight completely, one of my teammates noticed. He knew I could not see and was kind enough to lead me around that day and get me to a safe place until I recovered. He helped me to keep my secret. But each time it happened, I noticed it was taking longer and longer to regain my sight. I kept this condition hidden from the coaches and my mother for some time and kept playing.

Of course, my mother knew that something was going on. She brought me to see a doctor. After the doctor examined me, I was told that if I continued to play football, there would be life damaging results. Then, the doctor asked me to follow him into another room.

We entered what looked like a laboratory or research room. Many large glass jars and containers stood on shelves framing the borders of the room with an eerie presence. In some jars, I saw human fetuses suspended. Some of these fetuses had overly large heads.

Pointing a terrifying, shaky finger to the jars, the doctor gave me a stern look and said, "This is going to happen to you if you don't stop damaging your head!"

I believe my mother deliberately asked the doctor to scare me—to jolt some sense into me because she knew how stubborn I was—and it worked, for the moment anyway. I took a break from football, although, in the back of my mind, it was far from over.

On a humid day in June, my mother graduated with a degree from the university. As my brother and I sat, sweating in our stiff, wool suits, many people approached, greeting us with smiling and proud faces. They shook our hands and congratulated my mother. By witnessing her attend university and graduate with a degree, a path was cleared for us, one in which we could see ourselves with a future, something that was more difficult to envision before. My mother knew that by getting her degree—showing us what that looked like, and what that felt like—she was making a way for us to pursue higher learning. She knew that when a vision of the future can exist, it can become a reality.

We moved to New Jersey after my mother graduated. The football team at the high school there was also well-known. Many players went on to receive full scholarships to college. This was my big chance. That year I did well, and I was set to continue with the team for my senior year, when I got a call from my cousin back in Iowa.

"The coach asked me to call you," he said. "He wants you to come back to town and play for the basketball team. He says if you return, we'll win the state tournament."

This coach was the same man who opened the door for me at the community recreation center when I was nine years old. The man who witnessed me run around the track for eight hours straight. Because of that experience, almost a decade prior, he made it up in his mind—if I were to return and join the basketball team he was coaching, they could win the state championship.

This seemed a bit far-fetched.

First off—I did not play basketball; I played football. The sum of my experience with basketball was the street-games I played while hitch-hiking around the Midwest. Street ball has different rules and structure than organized team playing. Second—the high school team ranked so low, they were barely on the charts. To think that they could rise to the top in one season was unrealistic—some would say impossible.

I decided to return, not because of basketball, but because of my father. If I moved back to Iowa, I would move into his house. It was my last year of high school, and possibly the last chance I had to spend time with him. Already, I had missed out on so much time with him. I would not let this opportunity go by.

I went to tell my football coach that I was leaving.

"Son, are you sure? If you stay, I can pretty much guarantee you'll have a spot at a scholarship," he said.

"Thank you," I said, "but the reason I'm going back is to spend time with my father."

He paused at that. We both stood in silence, staring at our shoes, and then he nodded solemnly and said, "You go and do that, son. There is nothing more important than spending time with your father."

Big Time Small Town

When I arrived in Iowa, in the town where I was born—the news was out. The coach, in his enthusiasm, had the town excited and convinced that the high school basketball team was going to win the state championship. I was in a state of shock to find out that I was part of that equation. The evening after I arrived in town, my father handed me a suit and tie. We attended a banquet the coach had arranged. There were around two-hundred people, and I felt many eyes turned in my direction, like I was in the spotlight. From then on, the excitement and the hope of the community did not cease. There were more dinners, press meetings, and photos. As I walked down the street, strangers of all types waved, honked their horns, and yelled out words of encouragement. High school basketball, in those days, especially in this small town, was a big deal.

My relationship with basketball began when I was twelve. I learned that by standing on the side of the road and sticking my thumb out, hitchhiking, I could go anywhere I wanted—and so, that's what I did. Cleveland, Cincinnati, and even Chicago—I traveled all around the Midwest to play basketball in city parks. My parents never knew a thing.

I had noticed that all the money my friends made—working hard at those summer jobs—went into fixing their cars, paying for gas, and spending money on their girlfriends. I decided that was not for me.

"I'll be gone for the day, Mom." I'd say as I ran out the door.

My plan was to hitchhike to the next town over and play basketball all day.

"Ok, when will you be home?" she'd ask.

"I won't be back until this evening," I'd reply.

My mother was probably relieved. She thought that by going out, I was being social; I had friends and was getting out of the house. She saw this as a healthy thing for me, since I was usually so quiet and reserved. She never asked where I went. After leaving the house, I headed to the highway, stood on the side of the road, held my thumb out and waited for a car to pull over.

Sometimes, I'd go deep into New York City, to an area called the Bowery. The street folks sat around on milk crates beneath the freeway overpass, swapping war stories. I loved to sit with them and listen. Many of these men were highly educated, some with advanced degrees. I always thought that going to college, getting a diploma, guaranteed success in life. But I was learning it took more than that. Success was not something that was handed over on a piece of paper.

Listening to these men tell their stories was a great education. I learned more from their wisdom than I would by spending time going to parties, or doing the things most people my age were interested in. It changed my perspective of what defined success. I realized that there was much more involved in being human. I learned about making decisions, about honesty, betrayal, loyalty; about heartache, regret, delight, and defeat. I never told my parents how much I traveled. My mother would never have approved. But when I discovered hitch hiking, it was like I uncovered a wonderful secret. By the time I was a young adult, I had already seen much of the Midwest—playing street ball in nearly every major city.

When I arrived to play with the high school team my senior year in Cedar Rapids, though, in some ways, I was at a serious disadvantage. Street ball was much different from organized basketball. It was like learning a new language, a new system of playing and moving around the court. The other challenge (and advantage) was that the team in Cedar Rapids knew each other very well. They had been playing together since they were quite young. I was the outsider and did not know anyone. I had to learn the skills and patterns of every player and learn fast. I had a lot of work to do, but I was determined. The team was at a low status, ranked fourth from the bottom in the league. That we were going to go all the way to the top, to the state tournament was like saying that a team that typically lost most games was now going to win every game. It was a nearly impossible feat.

The second game we played was against a team who was notorious for scoring high. Not only had they beaten our team badly in the past, but they had outscored most teams in the entire league and in the state as well. As I looked around at my teammates' faces before the game, the fear in their eyes was clear. They were frozen. When we got out onto the court, they looked at the ball in their hands as if it were a foreign object. The emotion of fear has such a powerful effect on perspective—these terrifically capable athletes were stuck in their fear, incapable of using their amazing minds and bodies to do what they were already good at.

The team was disjointed, and not playing well at all in the first half of the game. I knew something had to change, or we were in trouble. I looked at my cousin, who was six foot seven.

I said through my mind to his, as calmly as I could, *everything is going to be ok...just pass me the ball.*

I knew that to help get the team out of the crushing grip of fear, they needed to have confidence. So we worked together—they passed me the ball, and I put it in the basket—we made basket after basket. Slowly, but steadily, as our score began to rise, I saw the vital strength come back. We began to wake up to our potential, and we began to play amazingly together as a team. We played well and won that game, but the most important thing was that the team saw for themselves what was possible—that we had the talent and the ability to play the game well. It was then that we, as a team, saw the dream, the vision, of making it to the top. From then on, our playing soared. We started winning one game, then another, and another. With each game, the confidence of the team grew stronger.

A unique form of communication developed between us. Soon, we no longer had to speak to one another in an audible language. Through one look, sometimes just a fast glance, I could say to another player something like, *open up the middle, let Larry through, or keep close to that player's right side.* It was this way through the whole tournament. We developed an internal mental language; and as a result, we worked beautifully together.

As this underdog team climbed to the top, enthusiasm from the fans that crowded the stadium grew to deafening roars of anticipation. Every game was sold out, or standing room only. To experience such immense crowds and stardom at such a young age was a life altering experience for us all.

Then the day came when we found ourselves standing on the court for the final game of the state championship. It was something that seemed impossible in the beginning, and still sometimes today, as I look back—it seems impossible—the odds of it. The game was broadcast nationally, and thousands of people were in the stands— easily the population of a small city.

During the state-championship games, I was not at my best physically. Something was wrong with my knee, but I didn't want anyone to know because I didn't want to have to stop playing in the middle of the tournament, and I knew that physically I could push through. I had what the doctor called "a floating body" in my knee area. A chip, a small piece of bone, was moving around beneath my skin. Sometimes it got stuck in the joint underneath my kneecap. When that happened, my leg would lock. By the time the last game came around, I was struggling, my energy was low. But we continued to work well together as a team to form strategies, communicating through our minds and through our hearts.

Our team was so strong together, that against all odds, we won the tournament and took home the title of state champions. We formed with one another an unbreakable bond for life. Several players on the team went on to professional careers as athletes. For each of us, that moment in time played a major part in our lives.

One of the biggest lessons I learned was in witnessing what was possible when a group of people came together with a common goal. I saw the beauty of people supporting each other to become their best. Consistently nurturing our areas of strength and helping each other in areas where strength was still growing. I saw the capacity of others, under overwhelming pressure, to achieve great heights, and through this, I could see the capacity and resilience in myself. My father was there in the stands, his support with me at every game.

After the season was over, the doctor advised that I have surgery on my knee to remove the bone chip. I had the floating body removed, and all was well. The following week after the game, I was back in school, getting around on crutches.

The doctor told me that if I had the surgery, there was a strong possibility I could not enlist in the military. He was correct. Months later, I received notice to report to the medical examiner prior to being drafted to Vietnam. Because of the floating body in my knee, I was spared from going to war.

This epic last year of high school was highlighted by the time I spent with my father. Quiet evenings in each other's company, eating sandwiches and watching TV. It was enough. Sometimes, he would try to convince me to leave the house. As a highly social person, especially when he was younger, he didn't understand why I wanted to stay in the house with him all the time.

"It's not normal for a young man to be sitting around the house. Go out and meet some friends," he urged.

So, reluctantly, I left the house to go out. He was not aware of how much I had already seen of the world, and how much I didn't care for the usual type of socializing that was popular with young people my age. I would rather be with him.

My father was a man of few words, and those words were always carefully measured. I never took them for granted. He guided, rather than instructed. It was important, he believed, for a person to *find himself,* and he gave me a lot of room along the way to do just that. Here and there, like a soft light through the trees, he offered his words of wisdom.

Once, during a basketball game, he witnessed me lose my temper. Something I thought was unfair happened on the court, and I was having a tough moment. The other team cast some ugly names in our direction. On the sidelines, I threw my towel to the floor, along with some heated words.

After the game, in a quiet but intense manner, my father said, "Son, you better learn to get a hold of that temper, otherwise you may as well quit with sports right now. Everyone is watching every move you make. They will see that anger as weakness and use it against you. You are a model for the team and for other young men who will follow in your footsteps."

I did not make any display of anger or frustration in sports from then on. His words always had a way of hitting deep.

The Transition

After high school, the attention that made me and the rest of the young men on the team, for a moment, celebrities—had vanished. It was time to move on, to go out into the world. I felt completely lost. The crowds, the attention, the warm and encouraging words—

were gone. In its place, the stillness after the excitement seemed stale. It was hard to know meaning, to know direction.

After graduating, right away, a prominent state university offered me a full scholarship to play football. But because of my inability to read, I could not accept.

When my father asked me why I turned down the opportunity, I could only reply, "It just didn't feel right."

There was some truth to that reply. Something didn't feel right about the situation. Although mostly, my reason to decline the scholarship had to do with my inability to read. The college, in their recruitment tactics, made outlandish offers to me. They offered to buy a house for my father, to give me a car, money and more. I knew there was something wrong with this. A year later, after I had turned down their offer, the university faced charges of illegal behavior in this area. It was a good thing, after all, that I had to turn my back on the deal.

Mostly, though, I felt I had to cover up my illiteracy and the shame I felt from it. This was the first of several scholarships that I would have to turn down because of my inability to read. Because of this, I thought that college was out of the picture. My options seemed dismal.

I decided to stay in town and get a job at the meat packing plant where my father worked. I could tell that my father was not happy about my decision, but silently, he supported me. Yet, to encourage me to consider other possibilities for my future, he worked some magic behind the scenes. In collaboration with others at the factory, he made certain they assigned me the worst, most vile tasks available at the meat plant. He wanted to make certain I did not last long.

Because of the responsibilities of supporting his family starting at a young age, my father could not follow his dream of going to college.

So, he passed this dream to me. He wished for me the opportunities he never had, and encouraged me (in few words) to move away from factory life, discouraging me from following in his footsteps. After struggling a couple of weeks within the worst areas of the factory, the choice was not difficult—I quit. My father, in his quiet way, was pleased to see me move on.

Through working at the factory, my father was not only able to support his family but could also help many people in the community. There was a large population of immigrant people, many from Czechoslovakia. He supported several shop owners financially to help them get established. Everywhere I went, whether or not I was with my father—the owners of bakeries, restaurants, and corner stores would greet me with the warmest smiles; offering sweets, sodas, or other goods.

I decided it was best to go back to Ohio. The memories of the woods and the pace of a small town seemed a good place to start and find a new direction. After so much attention in Iowa, after such intense focus with basketball, and feeling connected to a strong purpose—without it, I felt empty. I found a room to rent in the upper part of a house. For one month, all I did was sit in a chair, listen to music, and ricochet a tennis ball off the wall, catching it and throwing it again—over and over, day after day. This went on for several weeks. I was trying to find myself—Jim Nance, and bring him back, whoever he was.

Then one day, while out walking, I looked into a window and saw a woman. She was working with clay on a pottery wheel. Her hands manipulating the clay mound, pushing it down, pulling it up into forms and shapes. I had never seen this done before and it struck a curiosity in me that brought me out of my attic-ball-throwing room, and over to where she worked. The movement of the clay within her hands fascinated me. What started out as a pile of mud magically transformed into an object—a bowl, or a cup—something common, something I could recognize. I asked her if she would teach me. She told me that in order to understand the clay, I should throw one-hundred vessels every day. Also, I needed to clean and help keep the studio in order. I treated this as my new assignment.

So, each evening, I kicked the wheel, worked the clay, and formed a vessel with my hands. When I finished, I collapsed what I made, reworked the clay, and started again. I repeated this one-hundred times every night. Something about working with the clay offered me something that I needed desperately. It made way for a steady calmness and a way to feel grounded with myself. I went to her studio every evening. Overtime, feeling the earth between my fingers as it moved in a circular motion, molding and shaping it into form—I began to feel myself coming back into form, into my body, and reconnecting to my life.

Kung Fu

While playing basketball in a park one afternoon, I became distracted by a couple of guys practicing karate moves together on the grass. I knew that what they were doing was a martial art, but this was different. Never had I seen African Americans practice martial arts before. I set the basketball aside and went over to watch. As I watched their movements, so different from anything that I had ever been involved with, ideas started forming. This was something new—a new direction I could pursue.

Losing the intense focus that sports brought to my life had me longing for something similar, something that was physical and required an extreme level of discipline. Also, I thought that learning Karate may help me become an even better athlete. I had not given up yet on my dream of becoming a professional athlete. Soon, I started training and working out with a small group of African American martial artists. They were very serious about their training. A couple of them, later, became nationally recognized.

Starting at five in the morning, I went to the gym for five hours to work out and lift weights; I went to classes at the community college after that, and then back to the gym for five more hours in the evening. Around midnight, I went to the clay studio and threw one-hundred pots, and then to bed. Day after day, I followed this routine. I was only getting a few hours of sleep, but I became good at Karate, and quickly. After only one month, I worked as an instructor.

Together, our small practice group changed direction and decided to study and practice Kung Fu. These guys had been training together for a lot longer than I had, a few of them, since they were children. I had no prior training in martial arts. The coach would watch me and just shake his head in exasperation. He discouraged me from pursuing fighting and told me I was not any good at it. But after many hours of practicing every day, I became good enough to spar. This was when extraordinary things began to happen.

Naturally, I was a little nervous whenever we were about to fight. I had only been training for three months, compared to their many years. These guys were extraordinarily fast with their strikes. Some skills they had were dangerous, even lethal, and I knew that when we fought, they would not hold back—that was the kind of people they were. So, when I stepped onto the floor with them, I was facing something that could end my life.

One day, as we sparred, something mysterious took place. Suddenly, everything I saw began moving in slow motion. When my opponent went to strike, I saw his incremental movement—his balance shifted, his knee rose, and then, ever so slowly, his leg extended into a kick. It looked almost as if he was moving underwater, yet even more slowly.

While in that state of calm mind, as the strike came toward me, I raised my hand—and lightly, with only two fingers, I moved his foot aside. This happened again and again. It was like a slow-motion animation. I hardly had to move, only slightly, like flicking my fingers, and I could block every strike that my opponent made. Every time we fought, it was this way. If he tried to punch, I could gently shift my body to the side, and he'd completely miss me. If he kicked, I shifted the trajectory of his foot with barely a glance.

Once, as he came at me with, what could have been a lethal strike, his body flying powerfully through the air—again, things changed to slow-motion—I easily took a half-step to the side so instead of colliding into me, as he intended, nothing was there to receive his blow, and he landed on empty floor space. Surprised, he found me positioned behind him, where I could have easily struck. He would not have seen it coming. I realized then how potentially dangerous I had become as a martial artist. I did not wish to injure anyone, especially because with this newfound skill, I did not know how strong the repercussions of my strike might be. So, I never struck out aggressively but remained solely in a defensive stance—blocking and dodging the attacks.

In real time, my partner was moving much faster than the average human. He was so talented at Kung Fu that he had recently challenged and sparred with a Kung Fu Master—this fight became famous, going down in history, rumored as one event that led to the inception of a form that became known as mixed martial arts. This young man I sparred with was also quite hot-headed. Each time he failed to land a strike at me, he became more and more furious. He threw kicks and punches at me that burned with rage, while I remained in a defensive position, lightly batting them away or stepping aside.

I did not tell anyone about what was happening with the slow-motion vision. I was afraid that if I did, I would lose the ability. This gift, I knew, was saving my life. One day, we fought for thirty minutes, which is a very long time for Kung Fu. Usually, a match will only last about ten minutes. This time, our teacher was watching. He could not believe that he was seeing the same kid, who, three months earlier, was no good. My teacher knew that something out of the ordinary was taking place. So, he called his friend, a Kung Fu Master from China, and asked him to come and observe.

So, one day while we sparred, I noticed the Chinese Master was watching us from the side of the room. Once again, as we fought, I saw everything move in slow motion. I could see the movement they were about to make before they made it. When they struck out (ever so slowly), I stepped aside and shifted the direction of their strike with a touch of my finger. From an outside perspective, however, I believe it must have looked as though I was moving impossibly fast. The Chinese Master watched, and he knew what I was experiencing.

After every fight, though, tears fell from my eyes. I never knew why. The tears would just come. It was out of my control. Many times, my friends were there, ready with a towel for me. I grabbed the towel and put it to my face right away to hide the tears, hoping it looked as if I was merely wiping the sweat away. The Chinese Master saw this. He saw everything. After the match, he approached me.

"Everything is moving in slow motion for you, isn't it?" He asked right away, and in front of my sparring partners.

Seeing the startled look on my face, he went on.

"I don't know how it is you're able to do this technique. It is highly unusual—what you are doing. And in just three months you have learned this?" He shook his head with grave seriousness.

"Highly unusual!" he repeated. "Some people will train for many years, even their whole lives to reach this level. This is highly unusual."

After a long pause, he continued.

"There is nothing I can teach you. You need to study with someone so that you know how to use this skill appropriately. I am sorry, but there is no Master in this country who can teach you. Perhaps in China—but no one who speaks English. You must stop training in Kung Fu right away," he concluded, "or you will hurt yourself deeply. Your spirit is already getting hurt, and you are injuring it every time you spar. You must stop and walk away now."

What he said made a heavy impression on me.

The last thing he said was: "You should learn Qigong. Find a Qigong Master to teach you."

With a heavy heart, I packed up my Kung Fu locker. I knew it was the right thing to do. I knew that what this Master said was serious. I said goodbye, never to return to martial arts again.

Philly Bound

After Kung Fu had ended, I needed a change. I learned from my older brother that our former track coach was living in Philadelphia and involved in community work there. Perhaps I could join him and get a job. I called him and he said he could use the help. Soon, I headed toward a new life.

I was not completely unacquainted with big city living due to all the hitchhiking I did, but living in Philly was nothing I could have prepared for. On the first day, the old coach handed me a clipboard and sent me out to walk the neighborhood streets. My job was to talk to people and let them know where they could find resources, like food, medical care, or shelter. Community service, such as this, was a new thing, and people were wary, to say the least. I was some strange, big, new kid from Iowa wandering around with a clipboard. The community eyed me with suspicion.

People asked, "From where? Iowa? Isn't that where potatoes grow?"

It surprised them to know that African Americans lived in Iowa.

As I walked through heavy gang territory during my first month on the job, my life was threatened every day. Even the police were suspicious of me, and didn't understand, at first, what I was doing out there. It seemed like everywhere I went, when I looked over my shoulder, or down the block, there was a squad car following. People did not understand what someone like me was doing out there. I was like an alien being, yet one that looked familiar, strolling around the neighborhood and asking peculiar questions—like, did anyone need to see a dentist. After a time, it was clear to me that this work was not going anywhere. I would not be able to help anybody.

Then one day, while walking my usual route, I noticed some youngsters playing basketball in the park. Something in me just moved me toward that court. I set my clipboard down and picked up the ball. The guys on the court gave me a look that said, Ok, let's see what you got. You see, at this place in time, I was very good at the game, and physically fit. I had not only been playing street ball all over the Midwest for the past couple of years, but I had been training in Kung Fu and working out. I was fast and muscular. After we started to play, the other guys saw I had skills. I noticed they were looking at me in a new way, one that said—*You've been able to do this all along, but instead you're out there wandering around with a clipboard? Are you crazy?*

The more I played basketball in the neighborhoods, the more people talked about me in the community. The more people heard about me, the more they trusted me. One thing led to another. Soon, I had new contacts and acquaintances. I had no trouble on the street again. From then on, the first thing I did, if ever I ventured into an unknown neighborhood, was head straight for the basketball court. The kids, the old-timers, the parents—soon, they all knew who I was. I could finally talk to people. I gained their trust. Even the police started waving when they saw me.

All along, it was through the skills that I already possessed, the skills that carried me through school and kept me away from trouble—sports—that I was able to reach into the heart of this community. I did not imagine that basketball would take me in a direction like the one I found myself. A new avenue was opening—one in which I could be of service to others. My direction in life began to change.

One thing that struck me while living in the inner city was that there was no gym, no recreation center, or community building that was suited for indoor sports like basketball. Too many kids had nothing to do during the day, especially during the cold winter months. Many wandered the streets, often getting into trouble.

Then I noticed that there were churches everywhere. Most neighborhoods had at least two. A thought struck. *What if we could use these churches during the day for the kids?* Many had full gymnasiums already built in. As I told a fellow community worker my idea, I saw a light turn on behind his eyes. Just like me, he saw a universe of possibilities opening—something that could change things for these young folks in a substantial way.

So, we went around to the churches, talking to pastors and leaders. One church was especially enthusiastic about our proposal and invited us to begin the program right away at his church. After this initial support, other neighborhoods soon joined. The prospect of helping get the kids off the street and into something positive, something to help channel their energy, was motivating to the community—we had their support. It would not only help the kids, but the parents, the authorities, the families—everyone would benefit. We had to keep things clean. Everyone had to behave at their best. And everyone did.

The kids were so excited to have a place that was out of the winter cold—a place to play their beloved sport—there was never a problem. Utmost respect was given to the churches and the surrounding areas by the community. The blocks around the church became even better than before—no graffiti, and any unsavory business dealings moved elsewhere in respect for what we were doing, in respect for the kids.

Eventually, the public schools heard about the positive impact we were having with the kids. A school asked me to try working with some students they were having trouble with. These kids had seen and experienced more than any child should—unimaginable trauma. Most of the kids had challenges managing their emotions. Anger was always ready beneath the surface. After what they had been through, they trusted no one, and in return, no one wanted to work with them.

So, I went into the school carrying my basketball under my arm (which was usual in those days). Somehow, and by the grace of something much greater than myself, I could work with these kids. That same strange feeling would come into the room—that same feeling that I had many years before at nine years old, while I worked with the two little girls in Iowa. This sensation, this energy, would flow into the room with me. And it would move through us all, like a calming breeze, sweeping and gently soothing. It seemed the words that came from this subtle force affected the environment, as if my words moved through a filter as they left me—and it affected a shift in the kids. Something in their eyes became soft. When I saw the changes taking place, I knew everything was going to be alright.

Communication happened between the kids and I without a hitch. Chaos turned to stillness. Distractedness turned to trust. And then, with the aid of the ball, I could guide them to learn about what it meant to work together as a team, about listening and understanding, and about supporting one another. I never had a conflict in my sessions with the kids. Before long, I was working full time in several public schools with groups of children from every grade.

The D Word

Even though I did not tell anyone that I couldn't read, I believe many people who were close to me knew of my challenges. One of these people was my former track coach. I had been working with him on and off throughout the time I was in Philadelphia as we taught kids. During the summer months, I worked in the neighborhoods doing community service and playing basketball. In winter, I worked in the school system. Now, the coach was sending me to a new job. I would work alongside a professor, a scientist, who was helping a special group of kids. Before my first day of work, I was told very little about it.

When I arrived, I sat down to speak with the professor before the class began. She told me a story about a famous engineer: This man was an extraordinary mathematician who played a role in the development of new technologies for the automobile industry, among other areas, but the interesting thing was—he couldn't read. Somehow, because he proved able to solve mathematical problems of such huge magnitude, the world found a way. They made a system for him to communicate his genius. His ideas were so important, others knew that what was in his mind could help to benefit humanity. They created a technology to assist communication between this man and others—a language made of symbols and pictures that enabled him to draft his equations and designs. Because what he had was so important, an entire team of assistants were at his side, ready to record his every word.

As the professor relayed this story to me, she described something I had never heard of before—dyslexia. The mathematician in the story could not read because of this condition. She said that she had been studying this complex disorder for many years and believed she found a way to help children who struggled with it. She proved that by practicing a series of certain physical techniques, children with dyslexia could overcome their disability and learn to read.

As she described the symptoms and explained the effects, I knew right away that what she was describing was the very thing I had been living with all my life. I became excited upon hearing this information, but at the same time, afraid and still protective of my long-guarded secret. This heavy burden I had been carting around—and the main reason, I believed, that was holding me back from college, and ultimately, from living my dreams—was finally exposed.

I decided to share with her my secret. She was the first person who I told of my learning disability.

I said, trying to be relaxed as possible, "I think I may experience the same thing these kids are experiencing."

Of course, she may have already known. If she did, she only looked me in the eye and nodded her understanding.

Six hours per day, for several weeks, I spent my time helping the kids in her classes to do these special exercises. Much of the movement involved cross-lateral physical motion. Mostly, it was a repetitive series of simple tasks, such as reaching with one arm from the left side of the body, and then picking up an object on the right side. We also spent a good deal of time on our hands and knees, crawling across the floor.

One day, the professor wanted to introduce me to a parent of one kid in the class. He was sitting off to the side in our classroom, observing as we did the activities. I sat down next to him.

"Thank you," he said. "I am so glad it is you who is helping my son, because I know you can understand what he is going through."

Through our conversation, I learned that this man was the extraordinary engineer in the story that the professor shared before I started the class. Here I was, sitting with a man who had made significant contributions to the world through science and math. He, like me, could not read; and he, like me, was African American.

In later years, I learned that the professor I assisted in teaching these classes to kids made ground-breaking scientific discoveries during that time about dyslexia and the function of the brain. Her work later became widely known, helping to change the way we approach and understand this unique learning challenge. It was no accident that I had been able to not only meet her, but share in her work, helping the kids and helping myself at the same time.

After a school season of working with those children, doing the same cross-lateral exercises they did, day after day—placing things from right to left, left to right, crawling across the floor—I discovered one day, that I could read. It was a miracle.

Things Began

All my life, I believed in a story—I had no ability to read or write or pursue the path of academics. I believed the world was unavailable to me. I had resolved to accept this as the hard truth. Now, everything changed. I could read. I had wanted this for so long, now that I had it, I could barely contain my ambitious urges. If I could go to college, that meant that I could still pursue my dream of becoming a professional athlete—which meant everything.

Just then, another opportunity came my way. A regional college association formed, whose primary goal was to grant scholarships to young people who were involved with inner-city community work. Because of the work I had done with the kids in Philadelphia, I received recommendation to the program. We were paired with college students who tutored and prepared us to be college ready.

Along with others, I would learn to become more skilled with reading and writing and then apply for scholarships. This was my chance. My future was manifesting before my eyes.

One day, during the tutoring program, my instructor told me it was time to pick out my first full-length novel to read. Before me was a long table, with what seemed like hundreds of books spread across it. As my eyes scanned the surface of the table, a light blue color caught my eye. I looked closer and noticed the title of the book began with the same three letters of my first name, S-I-D—so I picked it up. The book was *Siddhartha*, by Herman Hesse. This book is the story of the life of Buddha, and the first book I read.

After completing the college-prep program, because of the extensive teaching and community work I had done, I was offered a full scholarship to an excellent school. It had only been only one year since I had uncovered, then resolved my dyslexia, and learned to read. Finally, I was on my way. I had a chance to make it in the world—to find success. Still, I was worried. *What if the dyslexia came back?*

The Mustang and The Voice

At 70 mph, the roads glittered with early-winter frost. I sat passenger in a black 1967 Mustang. My friend and I were traveling across the east coast, crossing through Pennsylvania, where winding roads cut with jagged stone wound through rolling country hills. Over the sides of the highway, within the deep valley below, house-sized boulders lay in place like ancient slumbering beasts.

We were headed back to college after a brief visit to the city. Out of the passenger seat window, I gazed down the steep cliffs at the sight below, mesmerized by the strange square boulders, placed like sculptures on display. When suddenly, I heard a voice. It was as clear as if someone was talking right into my ear.

It said in a calm tone, "Put your head down. Everything will be alright."

With no hesitation, I did just that.

Then: *Whoosh!* The car spun wildly, pin-wheeling across the ice-slick highway. Outside the window, all was a blur. Careening toward the side of the road and the treacherous drop-off, the corner of the car slammed into the guard-rail. The force of the impact threw me from the car. Bending the steel frame as I blasted through the passenger side window, I flew thirty feet through the air and skidded into the middle of the road.

Stunned, I stood up on the highway, brushing glass from my clothing. I barely had time to notice the battered mustang sitting in the lane behind me.

"Just stand up and stay where you are. Everything will be ok," the voice said.

I looked forward and saw a semi-truck headed straight for me at full speed. I had only seconds to react. But just as the mysterious voice instructed, I stood still.

The truck driver, upon seeing the crumpled mustang behind me in the same lane, veered to the other lane, flying past me. If I had not landed, after launching from the car window, within the same lane as the mustang, or if I had panicked and jumped into the other lane when I saw the truck, the driver, in a quick moment, would have had to choose between hitting me or crashing into the mustang with my friend still in the driver's seat. One of us, or all of us, could have lost our lives.

My friend was alright and was still sitting, shocked, in the driver's seat. I walked away with one injury—a small scratch on my thumb.

That night, I sat rocking in a chair on a porch, looking toward the pink-orange horizon as the sun set, thoughts percolating. *What or who was this voice that I heard just before the accident? This presence knew exactly what was going to happen. It helped me to survive.*

My mind was churning with possibilities. A spark was lit, the embers beginning to glow. *Where-how-who-what was this intelligence? How could I find it? Is it possible that there is a way to contact this source of wisdom?*

I had held onto the belief that my inability to read was my inability to function and be a success in the world. It was the story I adopted—the story of my inability. Then, when I finally learned to read, I thought that everything else in life would fall into place automatically. My future opportunities would wait at my doorstep, my life set in place. Now, since I experienced communication with a mysterious force that seemed to know exactly what was going to happen in the future—my mind flipped like a leaf in a sharp breeze.

I already knew I could learn through books, and through school, yet the voice that spoke to me before and during the car accident was proof that there was something more; something beyond the knowledge I was aware of. My mind was reeling. I knew my search was not over. Perhaps it had only just begun. Now there was something more; an intelligence—one which knew the answers.

I would find a way, I was certain, to connect to this knowledge. There was something in common with what I had discovered in Kung Fu—years earlier, when I experienced everything moving in slow motion—and the intelligence I experienced with the car accident. A new goal had placed itself in my life— to search for this connection. I recalled the Chinese Kung-Fu Master's final instruction: find a Qigong Master.

Little did I know then how long I would have to wait until I met such a person.

College Ball and the Wheel

I was so determined for success in school, after all that I had been through. That first year at college, I put enormous effort into my studies. One year after I read my first book, I found myself on the Dean's List. My dreams, though, were not held solely in the world of academics—there were sports and my ongoing goal of going pro.

After practicing Kung Fu and the experience with basketball on the east coast, I was physically in great shape. But I knew that if I really wanted to be successful on the college team, I needed to go beyond where I was. So, every day before the season started, I practiced dribbling the ball for four hours straight. In the locker room—around benches, down narrow halls, over, under, through—I dribbled the ball. If I could become so familiar with the basketball that it was like an extension of my own hand, only then, I decided, would I have an advantage in the game. I made the college team, but then tragically, during a game early in the season, I broke my thumb. I had been waiting for the moment for too long—to play collegiate basketball and show my skills. Now, for several excruciating weeks, I had to sit on the bench, watching, and wishing I could play.

Soon, though, my hand healed, and I was back in the game with a great explosion of energy. Every game, I excelled. Because of this, even though I had sat out for almost half the season, I was given an MVP (most valuable player) award. That summer, when I went to Iowa to visit my father, I brought my trophy. Strolling into his living room, I set it down on top of his TV. That's where he would want to put it, I knew, so he could see it all the time. I won't forget that day. His face lit up with a proud smile as I set the trophy down. Through me, I realize, he was able to achieve his dream of going to college. I knew it meant a great deal to him. This was another highly important reason I desired to go to school and get a degree— because of my father and all he had sacrificed for me.

In the beginning, at college, an alumnus interviewed me. He was working with the school to help new African American students adjust; also, he was a Rhodes scholar. When I told him I had some experience working with pottery, it caught his interest, and he proposed we work together to build a potter's wheel. The school had recently established a new community center. Its main purpose was to provide a place for African American students to gather, to build community.

So, we built a potter's wheel out of scrap materials. I designed it, and he helped gather the supplies. We set it up at the institute, and I started teaching others how to throw clay vessels. Before I knew it, it seemed like everyone was there at the wheel. There was great enthusiasm around working with the clay. Day and night, young people were going to the center to get on the wheel and work with their hands. There were times my phone rang in the middle of the night. Someone down at the center needed my help with the clay— asking me to come down and help him out with something he was making. So, of course, I would. I'd crawl out of bed and go down to the community center.

I didn't realize the full extent that working the clay—hands with earth, with water—provided something these young men direly needed. Much like what I had needed when I first began living on my own as a young adult. I needed purpose, something grounding me to the earth and to myself. I discovered a relationship with clay, or more like the clay discovered me. Working with earth, especially with the hands, gives way to a special relaxed concentration. This focus can, at least for a few moments, turn one's mind to an inward direction, away from the pressures and worries of the everyday grind. This type of focus can shift the mind from one perspective to another—to a life affirming focus. For these students, young African American men at college—a technique that provided a sense of connectedness and calm was needed. Stress can be at especially high levels in the collegiate environment. At the institute, on this little handmade, scrapped together wheel, these young people found a way to help themselves. Much later in life, I had the chance to hear from a student who had been part of this program.

He said it simply: "Being able to work with the clay changed everything."

The Turn to Türkiye

One night, after two years in college, tragedy struck. A few guys I had seen around campus were out partying one evening, which was, of course, normal for that age. One young man decided he wanted to cause trouble, to show off and pick a fight. He provoked me, and at first, I was successful in avoiding him. I tried to move away from the scene quickly; it was not hard to sense trouble in the air. But then I found myself backed into a corner, the aggression intensifying. I lost my cool, and in a flash, before I had a grasp on what was happening, I struck the student who had cornered me with a punch square to his jaw. To my shock, he fell over immediately, slumping to the ground, unconscious. Other students and friends were around, and they began attending to him, trying to wake him up. I was horrified. I may have seriously injured him. As a kid, I fought with others, in and out of school, quite regularly. But as I grew into maturity, the fights subsided. I had not seen that side of myself for many years. I vowed to myself right then—I would never ever again resort to violence, no matter what the situation.

The next morning, I heard the fellow was ok. That was the good news. The bad news was that I was going to be expelled from the school. The guy I hit happened to be the dean of students. I was certain then that my future, and everything I had worked so hard for, including my dream to play basketball professionally, was over. It was clear I had to leave.

Then, the day I packed my bags and was about to go—not knowing where, devastated at the prospect of my life in ruins—I got a call from my friend and roommate.

"Something came in the mail," he told me. "It looks important and official. And it's from Turkey!"

"Open it and read it to me!" I said.

It was an official letter inviting me to play on one of the Turkish basketball teams. *Unbelievable!* I thought, shocked. Of course, I said yes right away. I knew very little about Turkey (now Türkiye) besides what I learned in school and had never thought of playing basketball there. A fellow student, though, was Turkish, and we had become friends over the years. His family was in Istanbul, and soon he would go back. So, already, I had a connection. Suddenly, a path appeared for me where there was not one. There was no way that I would pass the opportunity by. Things were arranged quickly. I received an expedited passport, and soon found myself on a private plane, accompanied by a Turkish woman, on my way to a new life in a faraway land.

The sequence of events that happened next happened so fast, my thoughts could barely keep up. As the plane prepared to land, I looked to the woman who was accompanying me. We had been talking the entire plane ride, yet I still had so many questions. Her gentle demeanor comforted me, and I was feeling close to her. As the plane landed, she looked at me in a serious way. Tears were glistening in her eyes as she said a somber farewell. She seemed worried and nervous for me.

"Be careful," was all she said.

I had the feeling I would never see her again.

Standing at the top of the stairs, as the plane's doors opened, all I saw was a sea of flashing lights. I didn't know what was happening. Then, I realized that below and all around the airplane were reporters and cameras with flashbulbs taking photos, cheering, and smiling. *Were they here to see me?*

I did not know what a significant event my arrival in Turkey was. I was told that I was the first American (1971) to be recruited by a team to play basketball. The Turks were very serious about the sport, and many were fans of American ballplayers. It seemed I was an instant celebrity. There was a surreal quality to the scene that first night—I floated within a sea of flashing lights. I had landed in a historic moment. Swept from the plane, the flow of the crowd and the news cameras escorted me into my new life.

Sidney Basket and Miles Davis

My apartment in Turkey was all marble. Floor to ceiling—shiny white marble. I had seen nothing like it. All my clothes, suits, shoes—anything I wanted—was tailor made for me with the finest materials. And every club, every restaurant, everywhere I went, the servers rushed to clear a place for me. If there were no tables available, they created one. They brought dish after dish of the most incredible food, marching it in like a parade. I felt like royalty. This type of treatment, of course, was far different from what I had ever experienced most of my life. Absolutely everything was tended to with detail and precision while I lived in Turkey. It was like a dream.

It seemed everyone in the country knew who I was. Faces lit into smiles as I passed by.

"Sidney Basket!" they would call out.

I heard my name like a constant melody along the streets as I walked. It was clear my life was forever changed. *When I returned to the States, would I be returning to the same place that I left behind?*

When the team traveled to Poland to play a game, someone told me, "The whole country will watch you this evening!"

There were only two television stations in the country, and one of them would air the game—so this person really wasn't exaggerating. Still, I was a stranger in a strange land, wondering about where I had come from, and anticipating what I would have to go back to. Many eyes were on me, always. I felt a great amount of pressure to never do the wrong thing. I knew that if I made any mistake, it could not only be dangerous for me, but detrimental to athletes in the future who came to play for the Turkish teams. It was a great opportunity, and I was constantly aware of what, and of who I represented.

As we walked around downtown Warsaw before the game, a teammate tapped me on the shoulder.

"Look!" he said, pointing.

There, on the side of a ten-story building, was an enormous painting of the American jazz-great, Miles Davis. His image, along with his trumpet, spanned the width of the building. There I was—in a place so far from anything I knew—I was a young man from Iowa looking up at an eighty-foot-tall Miles Davis in Poland. Standing there, proud, and resolute—his dark expressive face, playing music for the world—for me. I discovered a sense of belonging at that moment, and it felt like something I had never known.

The Tone and Visne Suyu

Visne Suyu is a brilliant red cherry juice beverage served many places in Turkey. I liked to order it from a certain man on a certain street. He had a cart with equipment to make it with fresh cherries. Almost every day, I walked to his stand and bought a drink. We had little to say to one another, yet during the time I was there, we built a quiet way between us. He was always glad to see me, and with his eyes, said more to me than words could.

I noticed that while listening to conversations spoken in Turkish, I often heard a faint buzzing tone, like a constant murmuring accompanying the words, a low hum, its presence unwavering. If I adjusted my focus to hear that sound at the same time I listened to the Turkish language, I found I could understand what was being said. I was astonished. I kept doing this—as I listened to conversation; I tuned in to the humming tone at the same time—day after day. This became my language learning practice. As people spoke, I searched for the sound, and soon, after using this technique for a couple of months, I found I could speak the language myself. My Turkish friends were so pleased at this—and surprised.

Many wonderful opportunities came to me in Turkey, and quickly. I coached a women's collegiate basketball team, and since I could speak Turkish, someone even proposed that I consider becoming an ambassador. I made some good friends, and if I wanted, it seemed I had a future there. But early in the basketball season—the first play of the first game—I tripped and jammed my ankle, which then caused an injury to my back. I tried as best I could to manage and kept playing, but wasn't at my best. Soon, I had to use ice before the game and after, just to keep the swelling down. It wasn't getting any better. Finally, with advice from my Turkish friend, I boarded a plane back to the U.S. hoping to find some medical help. I never returned to Turkey.

Before I knew I was leaving, I went to get Visne Suyu drink from my favorite stand. My friend was there as usual, but when he handed the cherry drink to me, I noticed something was different. It was not as good as before; it wasn't the usual bright red color, and not as fresh as the drink he always served. I took the cup he handed me and took a hesitant sip. He gave me a look before I left that day—*this is it;* he seemed to say. *Something is about to change for you in a big way. Something that will make everything seem much different than you expect.*

Back Home?

After getting off the plane in New York city, I hitch-hiked to Iowa, then to Ohio, then made my way to Cincinnati, then back to Philadelphia. I went around in a circle—standing on the side of highways as traffic swarmed past, holding out my thumb, and climbing into the cars of strangers—only to land back in Cedar Rapids, Iowa again. I just couldn't stay in one place. If I tried, eventually an uncontrollable feeling, like a deep, persistent itch would overwhelm me, and I had to move on. I was claustrophobic to the world. The food, the conversation, the furniture—nothing was right. The only remedy, I felt, was to keep on moving. I didn't stay in one place for over twelve hours at a time. This period of restlessness lasted for two long weeks.

No one told me about culture shock. Even if I had been told, I don't know that I would have been able to identify it. All I knew, is that the world that I once knew was nothing I recognized—the place I believed to be my home no longer felt that way.

Finally, I went back to Philadelphia, where I was sure I could find work doing something I really loved—working with children. I planned to spend my days working, and spend my nights studying to finish my degree.

Cheese and the Blue Jeans Team

They called him Cheese. He was a fourteen-year-old genius, firecracker of a street-kid in Philadelphia. It was a mystery where he came from or where he went at the end of the day. It was clear he was used to doing whatever he needed to survive. I had known him since he was a young child, no taller than the doorknob on a door. Through the time I spent with him, and all the experience I had with kids, I could see that he was no ordinary kid. He was incredibly smart and soon he was a regular at the basketball court.

I kept an eye on him, though. He was like a wildcat—difficult to control, and quick. He would not listen to just anyone. But he was an exceptional ball player, and so, because his interest was in basketball, he had some respect for me, and I could get through to him in a positive way.

A couple of boys approached me one day after I had returned from Turkey. They knew I had played professional basketball while I was away, and asked if I would mentor them to prepare for a city-wide basketball tournament.

"This tournament is a pretty big deal," I said. "Many of these teams have been playing together for some time and organized ball is much different from street ball. You are going to have to work hard."

I felt like I had to give them a warning speech. There was a pause. None of the boys said a thing.

"How much time before the tournament starts?" I asked.

"Two weeks," Cheese said.

I knew Cheese was talented, and there was one other kid, a very tall guy, who was also formidable on the court. I had been watching them and saw that they played together well. Looking at the boys as they stood there waiting for my answer, I saw a seriousness in their faces. They were ready to work and to do what it took.

So, I agreed. I became Coach Nance.

Many of the teams competing in the tournament had been training together for years. They had professional coaches, fancy gear, and pro-ball players who stepped in to give pointers. These teams had money, which came in the style of flashy uniforms, expensive shoes, and matching towels. Our team had none of this. When the community and the parents found out that the boys didn't have uniforms, they showed up at practice one day with a pile of white t-shirts and magic markers. We spent the evening drawing names and numbers onto the T-shirts. Laughter, snacks, and hope were passed around. What we didn't have in dollars, the team made up for in spirit many times over.

That first game, our team stepped out on the court wearing their blue jeans and magic marker t-shirts. I had a feeling we were in for something more than what it seemed. This misfit group of boys was one of the most intelligent, eager, and talented I had ever worked with, and by the time the tournament came around, we had a way of working together that was uniquely ours. We felt confident and ready to show the world. The pure panache of our team quickly cut apart any jagged-edged jeers, or side-ways looks from other teams.

I had a special way of communicating with the boys during the games. It was like a chant. Through my voice and a unique rhythm and tone that we developed together, I guided them from the sidelines. Cheese and I had an especially fine connection. Cheese was not a tall person. Many players on the teams were the size of full-grown men. From a distance, they could easily pass as collegiate teams. Cheese was only about five and a half feet tall, but the way he shot the ball into the hoop was magical. With guys towering over him, their hands easily reaching over seven feet, Cheese could shoot the ball high over their reach and into the basket. I believe his brain held an extraordinary ability for mathematical precision. He launched the ball almost completely vertical as it left his hands—it flew in a long arch towards the sky, reaching heights no one foresaw. The court, the whole arena, became hushed as the ball vaulted through the expanse of the court—making its descent down, down—until magically falling through the exact center of the hoop in a *swoosh!* I felt like I was right there on the court with them; we moved together like wind and sky.

When it was Cheese's turn to take the ball to the hoop, I chanted from the side, "Do it! Do it! Do it! …Wait for it… NOW!" And then he made the shot. He never missed.

Game after game, we left players, and their coaches slack jawed as we slid through win after win. This raggedy band of kids poured their hearts out, showing themselves and the rest of the city there was nothing impossible.

The games turned over swiftly, and soon we found ourselves face to face with the final championship game. I will never forget it—there we were, pre-game, huddled close to one another in the locker room, about to step out onto the court and into the roar of the city, when something else, some other element started to sink in—it was the reality beyond the moment. That is—what lies after the game? I could see the question within every young face at that moment: *What does life look like after?*

As we sat in a circle together in that locker room before the last game, the tears formed. It wasn't the usual nervous excitement, but something deeper. I realized it was not just our opposing team that we would face that night—but the heaviness of reality. The truth, that all this goodness, all that we had with each other, would have to come to an end—and was going to end soon. The boys would be back into their old ways. Some of them, like Cheese, would be back out on the street, doing what they had to. The *then-whats* had taken hold—a weight I knew I could not hold back from them, however much I wanted to. I looked around at each one of their faces. I have never been so proud of a group of kids. And I let them know it.

We didn't win the game that night. But everyone—the families, the community, the coaches, all the kids—knew that we had achieved something wonderful. Parents met me with tears on the brink. They shook my hand at a loss for words.

After that night, I saw none of the boys again. I knew that some of them, including Cheese, would be back out on the street. I was nineteen years old then. I still think of them to this day, with profound gratitude, with pride, and with prayers.

The Boston Healer

As a young boy, people visited him at his parents' house. They came to ask permission to take him on a car ride, to be in his company for a few minutes. Those near him in his life discovered that while in his presence—sometimes for only a short period—their pain and discomfort would mysteriously disappear. From a very young age, he had an extraordinary gift of healing.

An African American who came from an upper-middle class Boston family—he grew to be a car mechanic by day, and a powerful healer at all times in between. His eccentric and loving character, along with his ability to heal, drew people from many paths of life to his three-story Boston house. From professors, to poets, from the rich and the poor—they all came to see him for help. The injuries I had from playing basketball were still giving me pain. My former coach introduced me to this well-known healer, hoping I may find some relief.

He carried a somewhat infamous reputation. It was, in part, because young, energetic people, mostly college-age kids, artists and idealists surrounded him (and it was the 70s). Sometimes, the house was a raucous scene. Loud music played over the stereo while young people cooked stew in the kitchen or lounged around in the living room. The Healer knew I was a serious person and not interested in the party life. So, throughout our time together, from 1972 to 1985, he kept that part of his life at a distance from me.

Mostly, we sat in his room and talked. Often, people came in for healing, and I witnessed him work. I wanted to learn about what he did. This was the first time I had ever thought about becoming a healer myself. Every so often, he would tell me things about his healing work.

"You'll see lad, one day you're going to do even greater things than I do." He said. "You will help many, many more people."

This was hard for me to believe. But he knew long before I did that one day I would be a healer.

There are many stories about this extraordinary man, but here, I will only tell a couple.

Once I witnessed this:

A woman was brought up to his room on the second story. Tied down onto a stretcher, two men wearing hospital attire carried her. Her arms and legs were bound, yet still, she attempted to lunge and flail about. They set her stretcher upright in the Healer's room and everyone found a place to sit. Apparently, this wasn't the first time the hospital men had visited the Healer. They were familiar with the house. They knew where they were going and acted as if what they were doing was part of a usual routine. Whatever was about to happen, all those present seemed to know what to expect.

The Healer was calm as usual, mostly ignoring the commotion, and as they set the woman down, he stayed where he was—lying in his bed, while some show flickered idly on the television. But, as I sat there, I noticed a shift. A peculiar sensation overwhelmed the room in a matter of minutes. It was as if gravity had increased. The pressure grew and grew. The air all around us was heavy with an electrified, all-encompassing pressure. Then suddenly, everyone in the entire room slumped over at once asleep; everyone except for the woman tied to the stretcher, me, and the Healer.

The Healer did not move; he didn't seem to be *doing* anything. He just sat there across from the woman on the stretcher. All was silent for some time, and I fought with the heavy feeling of sleep. I may have nodded off, but I am not sure. The next thing I knew, the woman tied to the hospital stretcher was speaking. She and the Healer were having a normal conversation, like two old friends— nothing strange.

In a short time, the energy shifted again, and the pressure in the room lifted. Everyone woke up simultaneously, as if on cue. Some had to pick themselves off the floor, yet no one seemed alarmed. As they awoke, they found the young woman, now unbound, sitting calmly, having a conversation with the Healer. The hospital workers and the woman gathered themselves, packing their things, as if it was a normal, everyday event—as if they had just finished with a Sunday picnic. The medics folded up the stretcher, which they no longer needed, and they drove off together, everyone chatting amiably like pals.

Another time: A man came to the healer. He had been diagnosed with a terminal illness. I sat in the room as the man told his story.

After listening, the Healer turned to me and said, "You do it, lad. You heal him. Just go over to him and wave your hands around."

I could hardly believe what he was telling me. I had never done anything like it. But I stood up and went over to the man. For several minutes, as the healer instructed, I stood near the man and waved my hands.

After about twenty minutes the man left. A few days later, following a visit to the doctor and more testing, he returned. The hospital informed him that the illness was completely gone. He was ecstatic as he told his story. The doctors, bewildered, could not find any evidence of the previously diagnosed terminal illness. Overjoyed by this news, he invited me to go back with him to the town where he lived. He told me that there were many wealthy people who would pay me well to do what I did. The Healer told me it was best to decline this offer, and I followed his advice.

This was my first experience with healing energy, and I really did not know how or what had happened. It would be many years before I found the opportunity to learn more.

One of the most amazing things that happened through my association with this Boston Healer, was that my perspective changed. When I first went to see him, my goal was to heal my physical injuries from basketball. I needed to heal my damaged body and was searching for a way. Mostly though, the reason I wanted to heal these injuries was so that I could get back to playing sports. All along, that was my underlying goal. For almost as long as I could remember, my focus in life was to pursue sports.

On the first day I met the healer, I asked him if I could continue to play basketball.

He paused a moment, looking off at an unseen distance, and then in a casual manner, he replied, "Sure, you can do that."

But then I noticed, almost right away after I returned from seeing him, that something had changed in me. It was subtle at first. I got ready to go out one evening and play basketball, when I found I was really dragging my feet to get out the door. This was unusual for me. Normally, I would rush around, excited to get to the court and play as soon as possible. But I felt this persistent feeling that lay beneath my thoughts—for the first time, I found I did not really want to go.

This pattern continued through the weeks that followed. Things would pop up that got in the way of me going out to play. And then I began to notice the athletes around me. It was like I was seeing them for the first time. I discovered that many of these guys cared little about living a healthy lifestyle. Many of them were interested in things that I didn't want to have any part of—like nightlife and other destructive patterns. The more I saw, the more I was disinterested, and the more I felt like pushing away from my association with them and with basketball all together. Eventually, I realized—it was time to leave my dream of professional sports. My body had had enough, and the unhealthy lifestyle I witnessed in the people around me was not the direction I wanted to pursue.

Years later, after becoming a healer myself, I realized that one of the greatest gifts that this Boston Healer gave to me was not in healing my injured body, but in healing my perspective. I was able to adjust my focus in life and begin the process of healing my spirit. Through these initial stages, and in the years that followed, I began to learn more about the power of perspective and the profound impact it had on one's life.

Over the next twelve years, I continued to visit the Healer, traveling to Boston every summer, and staying for a couple of weeks at a time. There was more I needed to know about this mysterious healing force.

Moving On

After I finished my degree, the time came for me to make a big decision—to stay or to leave Philadelphia. So much had happened in that city, so many great and extraordinary things. I went from wandering the streets with a clipboard—a fresh-from-Iowa kid— to organizing community programs, to teaching in the schools, to overcoming dyslexia; and now I was a college graduate. Most importantly, I was able to move beyond my long-time goal of being an athlete. So much of my life, up to this point, revolved around that aspiration. Now, I could build a new story for my future.

I loved the kids I had been working with in the city. Many I had known since they were small. I had an attachment to them, and it was hard to let go. As I was weighing out these thoughts and plans one evening, a man appeared before me. He was an older fellow and a prominent member of the community. We stood together in the early evening and chatted as he chain-smoked cigarettes. Glancing at me now and then from the sides of his eyes, it seemed he sensed my every thought.

"You had a good run. You've been lucky. How many young men

could come out here onto the streets of Philly and survive? And from Iowa!" He shook his head and inspected the pavement.

"No, not many," he continued. "You've been fortunate, son. But now, you should go, else you'll be like me, still here. I've been shot three times—and I'm lucky. You see, what these kids really need is to see is someone like you—here to do a good thing, and then gone—moving on to do other, greater good-things. They need this example. They need to see what is possible. Then perhaps someday, they too can see a way for themselves—out of the routine, off the streets. By seeing you leave, they may see they have options—like you. This is what you should give to them. Just leave." He stamped out his cigarette, told me good luck, and walked away.

I knew in my heart he was right. The best gift I could give these kids was to walk away. And so, without any drawn-out farewells, I left Philadelphia.

From Drapes to Zen

What came to me in Cincinnati looked like this: A well-paying corporate job, a steady future, a life of comforts. I couldn't have imagined this kind of story for myself. After my time on the east coast, dealing every day with the hard reality of kids on the street and poverty—going from there, to a work-a-day job stocking shelves and running orders, was like a piece of cake delivered on a silver platter. I was happy to be there, and happy to be alive. Spending days chatting with the old ladies in the stockrooms, I kept a polite manner and was helpful in any way I could be. Soon, I had an excellent reputation at the company and somehow, in hardly any time at all, I found myself working alongside the top buyers in the corporation—filling million-dollar orders and standing on the sidelines of big-deal decisions. I, in no way, imagined myself in this position. What I thought was just a temporary warehouse job, until I found something steadier, turned into a full sales position.

And then in no time, I found myself having lunch with the top executives. They were grooming me into a role that would place me as the buyer in the largest market for drapery in the Midwest.

In many ways, I found the corporate world interesting. I learned about marketing, and the predictability of consumers. I was told that if I stayed with the company, I would be next in line for a six-figure position. For many, this might sound like a dream come true; it looked like a picture of success. Yet something within was pulling me in another direction. I could easily stay in Cincinnati and live an upper middle-class life. And I was grateful for all I had. I had stylish furniture, fine suits and enjoyed a fair amount of luxury and ease, and complimentary steak dinners. But something was telling me to go another way. I just didn't know what that looked like yet.

A memory visited me one day as I was out walking. It was a scene from my days as a kid in Yellow Springs, where I spent time in the woods and rolling hills. It was the day my mother took me to visit the Zen nun in her house made of dirt. I recalled the feeling that came over me as I sat in her hut, as steam curled through the air from boiling tea water—that strange and quiet feeling as the nun moved—her hands, the small clay pots, smoke dancing in the candlelight. With these memories flowing through my mind, I wandered into a bookstore in downtown Cincinnati. I found myself in the Zen section, staring blankly at the bookshelves in front of me. Something was leading me—a book caught my eye, and I reached for it. Simultaneously, I noticed another hand, a more delicate hand, reaching for the same book. Time slowed. Before I could touch it, I watched as the other hand, smaller and paler than mine, took the book from the shelf. I turned to see an older woman with shining bright white hair. A glow, like light, hovered around her. *I gasped silently. I was transported to a scene from my early childhood. A darkened room. Tears. A foreign smell and a strange bed. The little golden-haired girl.* Standing before me was the same woman I saw in Iowa when I was a young boy. She stood in the dark room as I cried over being separated from my parents. Now, standing beside me in the bookstore, looking as if she had never aged, she smiled and held the book out to me.

"Here, you take it," she said. "You're going to need this more than I will."

The book was *Zen Mind, Beginners Mind*, by Suzuki Roshi. It became a very important book in my life, and one which I still have on my shelf to this day.

During summers, when I visited the Healer in Boston, I often stayed in an octagon shaped room. The house, perched high atop a hill overlooking the town, they say, was the oldest in Cambridge. I loved to wake up early and catch the sunrise as it lit the urban scene.

Many eccentric people stayed in this unique house. The man who owned it was head of a department at one of the prestigious universities in the area, and enjoyed the lively company of scholars, artists, and intellectuals who frequented the city. Because of my association with the Healer, the octagon room was always available for me, and I was treated with great kindness.

One day, in conversation with someone at the house, I mentioned I was interested in studying Zen. There happened to be a guest staying who was a student of Zen. After being introduced, he advised me—rather than trekking all the way to California as I had planned, where there was a well-known Zen monk—to go instead to Minneapolis, Minnesota. There was a Zen master by the name of Katagiri. By going to study with him, I would have a better chance of getting to speak with the Roshi directly, compared to the popular west coast location, where there were hundreds of students vying to have a moment with their teacher. In Minneapolis, there was a much smaller community. This man, who was friends with the Roshi, called to tell him I was on my way. So, that was it. I was on my way to Minneapolis to find Katagiri and Zen.

Fortunes Path

Each day, I found money lying on the ground.

Walking the pathway around a beautiful chain of lakes in Minneapolis—ten-, or twenty-dollar bills were consistently in my path. Every day there was money waiting for me. I could hardly believe my luck. When each day for about a week in succession, I found bills on the ground; I started to get suspicious. I tried an experiment one day, and didn't pick the dollar bill up right away. Instead, I left it where it was, and I walked past it. Sitting on a nearby bench, watching, waiting, I tried to look busy. The extraordinary thing was—it seemed no one else could see the money. I observed the scene, bewildered, as people walked right by it—again and again. The money lay in plain view, yet not anyone altered their step in the least. Eventually, I gave in, tired of waiting, and picked it up. Even though I felt a little uncomfortable finding this money so often, it was helpful because I did not have employment yet.

I phoned my father to tell him about the money on the ground.

After hearing the story, he said in a serious tone, "Son, you should never leave that place. Something good is waiting for you there."

The Rōshi and The Wolf

When I arrived in Minneapolis, right away, I went to the Zen Center. Katagiri Rōshi, the Zen Master from Japan, greeted me warmly. As he introduced me to his students, he referred to me as "his friend." I noticed that there were a few befuddled expressions from his students. Katagiri and I had only just met, but because he told the group that I was his friend, it caused a stir of curiosity. This was the way Katagiri was—intelligent and kind. He always treated me as a friend and an honored guest.

Meditation was agonizingly painful for me. Still, I went to the Zen center every day to practice. Whether I sat in a chair, or on the floor, didn't seem to matter—the pain was nearly unbearable. I knew it had something to do with the injuries I accumulated through my years in sports. But I was determined to keep trying. So, through the bells, the incense, and the chanting, I moaned and groaned and shifted my body around through each painful session. The noises and distraction I brought were annoying the other students; their patience was being pushed to the very edge of their meditation cushions.

Katagiri Rōshi, noticing this, told an ancient story:

"There were four horses. The first horse had only to see the whip, and he would take action. Another horse could take the direction from his master with only a gentle nudge, and the horse turned on course. The third horse, though, needed a sharp slap to go in the right direction. But the fourth horse, before he could make that same turn, had to be whipped until the sting of the blow reached into his bones. Now I ask you, to which of these horses do you think the Buddha offers his grace and compassion most?"

One day, during a break at the Zen Center, I was outside in the beautiful, partly wooded back yard when I saw a magnificent dog. This huge, white dog was watching me with its golden eyes from the edge of the woods. When our eyes met, he made bowing and leaping movements, like he wanted to play. So, I obliged, and we chased each other around the trees. I had very little experience with dogs. My grandmother had several, and I was around them when I was a child, but they didn't interact often with anyone except my grandmother, who could be quite fierce.

We were having fun, the dog and I, running around in the grass, when I noticed one of the other students standing at the side of the yard. He was motioning to me, waving his hands in a hurried way, directing me to come toward him. I didn't understand why he didn't just come over to me if he had something important to say. I told the dog I would be right back, and he gave me a funny look like, *Oh no you won't.*

"Jim," my friend whisper-yelled as I walked across the yard, "that is no dog!"

"What?" I asked, surprised.

"That's a wolf!" he said.

When I looked back to the woods where I left him, the golden-eyed dog-wolf had vanished. I never saw him again.

Still Searching

For many years, I had been searching for a Qigong Master. In every town I stayed—from the east coast to the Midwest—I visited Tai Chi studios, and martial arts dojos, asking, speaking to teachers and students, yet no one had ever heard of a Qigong teacher in the U.S. What the Kung-Fu Master instructed when I was nineteen, to find a Qigong Master, was still on my mind. I was aching to find someone who might know the answers to the mysteries I had experienced. Since the car accident and the voice that guided me, I was even more determined. I would keep searching until I found someone, someday, to teach me Qigong. Once again, I felt pulled to continue to follow the mystery, searching for answers.

Because the pain was unrelenting, and I saw no improvement on the horizon, eventually, I had to stop practicing meditation at the Zen Center. Instead, once a week, I went to visit and chat with Katagiri Rōshi. This continued for some time. Later, toward the end of his life, when he became ill, he called me for help with healing. I was not yet a healer (that I was aware of) and did not have the skills needed to help him completely. Katagiri knew, though, before

I did, that the healing path was in my future, and he helped ignite that spark within me—the spark of a healing direction. I cherish those quiet moments that I was fortunate to have had with this very special, gentle, and wise teacher.

The Eye in the Sky

I was married in 1982, and soon after, we began to plan for a trip to Africa. We intended to travel for one year on the continent. So, I worked three jobs to save up money—a part time teacher at an alternative school for kids, an overnight job working at a home for people with mental challenges, and then I added a paper route delivery in the early morning. After about one year of both of us working and saving, we felt we were ready to go.

While alone on a long drive from Iowa to Minnesota, after visiting my father, this thought came to me: *What am I going to do in Africa?* You may be thinking that this was a topic I should have already put some thought into by this point, but I was so focused on the *how* that I had put no time into the *why*. I decided I needed to have a plan of my own. I needed a purpose for this trip, a direction. As I continued driving down the flat expanse of roadway—corn and soy fields on either side as vast as the sea—I let these thoughts float through my mind. I realized that the same interest, a search for spiritual understanding, had been with me always, moving me along, letting me know where to go next. I contemplated the possibility of exploring spirituality in Africa.

As soon as the thought came to me, I knew it was the right direction. I would seek—throughout travels across the continent of Africa— spiritual people, wise people, medicine people, and learn from them what I could. Driving along as these thoughts formed, suddenly, I became incredibly sleepy. I couldn't shake the heavy exhaustion any longer, so I pulled over to the side of the road. Stepping out of the car, a vision stretched across the sky before me.

At first, I thought I must be sleeping and dreaming, but that was not the case. My car sat on the side of the highway, where I had pulled over. I reached out to pat the top of the car just to sure. I was not sleeping. I was standing on the shoulder, on an Iowa road, looking up at the sky. And there in the center of the sky, looking back at me, was a gigantic eyeball—as clear as anything. It was staring directly at me. Next, the form of a woman appeared. Her proportions were also enormous. A deep copper color covered her nude body, and her hair separated into great locks. Just as I had the thought, *this can't be real*—the eye in the sky winked at me, and the woman flew across the horizon, leading with an outstretched arm as tremendous wings extended behind her.

Just then, a car was about to pass me on the highway. I thought, *surely now this image will disappear.* But it did not. The car passed, blind to the event at hand. I lifted my gaze back to the sky to find the giant, winged woman continuing her pathway across the blue expanse. The great eyeball continued to watch me. Eventually, it was time to leave. I had been standing there so long, if I stayed any longer, I was likely to attract unfavorable attention. As I got back into my car and drove away, only then did the vision in the sky fade. It slowly dimmed, like a disbursing mist, and then it was gone.

Africa came to me like this: It was always there—just waiting.

The Gift of Gifts

Before going to the great continent of Africa, we decided it would be a smart plan to find out as much as we could from African people who were living in the States. So, we called the local university and asked if they knew of any African students in the area who would talk to us about their home country. Before long, a young man from Zimbabwe contacted us. Over dinner, at a place of his choice, we told him how excited we were to visit his country, asking him questions like: Where should we visit? What foods should we eat? He seemed delighted we were so interested in his homeland and was happy to tell us all we wanted to know. He told us the best dishes to eat and the best areas to explore. At the end of our time together, we asked the student if there was some small gift he would like us to deliver to his family while we were in Africa. A huge smile came over him.

"Yes! Of course!" He replied.

And that's when it began.

Over the next several weeks, we met with many more students from different countries in Africa. After the first meeting, we embraced the habit of offering to bring a gift back to their families. We offered this to every student we met. The students were so happy, some nearly jumped from their seats with surprise and excitement—they did not hesitate to give us small packages, along with the addresses of their families.

As I boarded the plane, I carried over my shoulder a huge duffle bag full of gifts for all the students' families. I brought hardly anything else with me. Delivering these gifts meant we would visit nearly every country in Africa. An amazing thing, I found, about this duffle bag full of gifts, is that, not one time—through all the trains, the buses, the wild taxi rides—not once did anyone try to take anything from the bag; no one even attempted to open it. It was as if there was a beautiful, incorruptible protection over the precious cargo.

The impact that these gifts had on the families in Africa was something I could not have expected. After we located the family's address, we mapped out the directions. When we found the house, or apartment, we simply walked up and knocked on the door. As the door opened, we faced mothers, fathers, brothers—eventually the whole family, and sometimes the whole village. Initially, there was some confusion as we relayed our story, and sometimes there was apprehension. Then, as we held out the gift, adorned with the familiar handwriting of their child, any confusion quickly transformed into surprise, and then finally, to great joy.

We witnessed many tear-filled moments between family members as we delivered those small gifts. It meant more to them than we could possibly know—a message from their beloved daughter or son, living so far away, in a strange land—a message that they were ok. At these times, as tears sparkled, it felt as if the whole of Africa was embracing us.

Exuberance followed the initial shock as we introduced ourselves, usually accompanied by an invitation to stay in the family home. A feast was prepared. We enjoyed some of the most delicious food I have ever had in my life. For the next several days, we were introduced to the village or community as honored guests. We felt like royalty. They often wanted us to stay for several weeks, but usually we stayed just a few days.

"We have so many gifts to deliver," we tried to explain.

Yet, always, it was hard to leave. There would be more tears, more embraces, and, of course, more great food.

Our first stop was in Kenya. After we arrived, the first thing we wanted to do was to find something to eat. The restaurant we found, to our surprise, was an Indian restaurant. Everything in the restaurant was red—the walls, the chairs, the cooks, the servers; they all wore red. After we ate, the restaurant owner came over, curious about where we were going. We told him we were headed to Kisumu.

With a puzzled look on his face, he said, "This is a very small place. Do you know anyone there?"

When we told him who we were visiting, his face lit up immediately. He knew exactly where we were going. The person we were visiting was highly respected. Many people knew her. He then told us everything we needed to know about getting there—who to speak to, and where to stay. This was to be the tone of our entire trip. If there was anything we needed to know, often, someone would show up with the information or offer to guide us. It was as if people already knew what we were seeking before we had to ask. Sometimes the things we thought about would appear in just moments after the thought occurred. It was sometimes frightening.

One day, my wife casually mused, "I wonder what it would be like to see lightning strike a tree."

The next day, that's what happened. Lightning struck a tree right in front of us. In one terrifying hit, as it exploded into fiery splinters and charred bits, from then on, we decided, at least while we were in Africa, we had to be careful about our thoughts.

Kisumu

When we arrived and met the woman who would receive the first gift, she greeted us with warmth and graciousness. She invited us to stay with her in her house for a time.

The next day, she told us in a casual way, "I am going to take you somewhere. There are some people who would like to meet you."

I imagined a picnic or a dinner—some food, a few people, something low key. But when we arrived, after driving a distance, there were no less than three hundred people waiting for us in a wide, open field. We walked into the field, where we found seats set for us. The people formed a long line and, one after another, they came forward to shake our hands and welcome us to Africa. The whole town, and people from villages from around the area, were all there to see us—everyone smiling, hugging, happy, embracing us gently. I have never felt so welcomed, so honored.

"They heard about what you are doing—delivering the gifts across the continent—and they all wanted to meet you." Our host said.

For the rest of our stay in Kisumu, we were treated specially. We were shown the beauty of the land. It was a wondrous time, and hard to leave.

One of our last visits in this area was to see our host's mother. She was a renowned healer and head of the local hospital. She was busy with a special task—her husband was nearing the end of his life. In their tradition, during the time at the end of life, the husband and wife spend every day together, taking turns telling each other stories—all the wonderful stories of their lives together. She sat by his side day and night. They had been together for a very long time, so they had many stories to tell.

She came out of the tent where she sat beside her husband and met with us briefly. Already, she had heard about us from the community, also she had heard that I was a teacher.

"Come back to Kisumu and teach," she told me. "You will have a place to stay here." I knew that if I returned, I would learn a great deal from this wise healer.

After leaving Kisumu and many tearful goodbyes, we got on a bus to Mombasa. The bus was severely crowded—this was normal. Three to four people sat on each seat, children and babies on laps, while still others stood in the aisle. I was sitting next to a woman and her young daughter when I noticed something strange was happening in the front of the bus. The entire surface of the windshield was vibrating and shuttering violently. Suddenly, within seconds of noticing it, the entire piece of glass spanning the width of the bus shattered with an explosive force into hundreds of tiny pieces. The shards shot out like pellets into the bus, scattering across the people inside. Somehow, just before the explosion, I stood up and turned my back, shielding the woman and her child who sat beside me from the bombarding pieces of glass. It showered over my back, sticking into the fabric, and some piercing into my skin. The bus pulled to the side of the road, where we got off for a moment. Some people on the bus helped to brush the glass off my back and shake out my clothing. When I got back on the usually noisy and lively bus, everyone was silent, unmoving. The young mother with the child gave me a look of gratitude I will not forget.

The Final Delivery

As chance allowed, the last gift that we had to deliver was from one of the first students we met with back in the United States— a young man from Zimbabwe.

After receiving the gift, his father smiled and shook his head, looking at the empty, over-sized duffle bag in my hand.

"You delivered all these gifts to Africa?" He laughed. "You left as a slave and came back as Santa Claus!"

This man was prominent in the community, a leader.

"Whatever it is that you want to do, I will see that it happens," he said.

When I told him I wanted to meet a healer, a huge grin crossed his face as he and his son exchanged glances.

"I know just the person," he said.

The indigenous medicine people of Zimbabwe are well known. It was said that they had extraordinary, or super-human gifts—some could see into the future, others were healers. Our friend arranged a meeting for us with one of these healers.

The healer lived in a dome shaped house. A small fire burned out front, and inside, a simple cloth divided the room. He sat on the one side of the cloth; we sat on the other, and could not see him. The language he spoke was so ancient, it took a succession of four different translators to relay his words to us. He would say something, then out of a line of men—the first one would translate it into another African language, the next would translate from that language, then another, until finally it was translated to us in English. They said this language was at least six thousand years old.

The sound of his voice was unlike anything I have ever heard in my life—like metal grinding on stone, or some ancient beast's growling breath; like the gravely depths of the earth exhaling.

"You are like me," he said. "You are already a healer, but you don't know it yet."

Seeing me in the future, he described certain events. If I stayed there, in Africa, and studied, he said I would be like him. He felt it was my destiny to follow the path of a medicine person, but there was no way to do that in the United States. In a couple of days, he informed me, I would go through a ceremony with others. Then he gave me a list of things I needed to do to prepare. So, I followed his instruction.

In my life, I feel I have had a number of baptisms, yet all were only symbolic—until this one.

Baptism

My baptizing as a child took place within a great steel cylindrical tub. As the preacher dunked my eight-year-old head back into the water, I opened my eyes (which was not what I was supposed to do). And as I went under, I saw another figure standing behind the preacher, one who was not there before. He was standing in the water, dressed in white cloth. Later, I asked my young friend—there beside me, waiting his turn to be dunked—if he saw this mysterious figure. He said he had not.

Here I was, sixteen years later, in Zimbabwe, looking for healing, and about to take part in an ancient ritual, one that I knew nothing about.

Through the years, we collect experiences. We make connections with others, and these connections can last an eternity. These connections have a huge impact on our spirit. Just one aspect of our experience in this life can influence the whole our life. For example, we now understand how positive emotions, such as joy and happiness, have an impact on our lives. We also know, through science, that every cell in our body can transform, can change permanently from such energetic experiences. Also, not only are we affected by what we see, touch, and do in this life, but we are changed and influenced by our mother's experience, our grandfather's—going on and on through time. What is part of our blood, part of our cells, our DNA is in some form, information, and this information is shaped by our experiences.

I have discovered that over time, through our spirit's accumulative experiences, we need to cleanse and clear our energy. There are many elements which make up who we are as energetic beings— environment, experiences, and relations are a few. This is part of what happens in a baptism. It is a cleansing ritual.

The Ceremony and the Escort

Harmony and rhythm wove together in the thick heat as the people stood together fingering their mbira thumb pianos—metallic, melodic resonance, mixing with light and the drums' beat. The music creates such a lulling spell, wild animals have been known to gather near and listen.

I was directed to sit down and to close my eyes. A man approached and began touching the crown of my head with careful and soft tapping movements, soft as bird wings. I could not tell what he was doing but felt his hands moving across the crown of my forehead, making small, precise, rapid tapping movements. Then I saw a cloth decorated with bright red spots (which I soon realized was my blood) tossed to the ground. I was being prepared for the ceremony and tattooed with short, vertical cuts patterned in a line across the front of my head.

Dancing, music, drums—voices in harmony—and the dusty, hot earth. An ancient smell—metal, minerals, earth, and smoke transported my senses. Many bodies surrounded me, and we moved together as one body. Music filled every particle of air, pushing us forward. The procession led to the water hole. Low from drought, it was only a couple of feet deep. Standing, my legs in the water. One man, maybe two beside me—*the man in white robes?*

A cup held to my lips. Bitter medicine. Drinking it down. Falling into darkness—falling, falling, unending dark—pulling me further and further down, toward the infinite blackness. I fell into the dark water. I lost consciousness.

Suddenly, powerful arms were pulling me back—back to the present, back within my body.

God's gonna trouble the water.

This line from an old gospel song says that God's presence is going to be there in that water, in that baptism, in that transformation. And that water is going to cleanse you of all spiritual limitations—your past, and all that holds you back—and grant you clarity toward a limitless spiritual path for your future. When the ceremony ended, I was a new person, though I did not yet know how.

The air felt wonderful across my skin that evening after the ceremony, and I had a strong urge to go on a walk by myself. I really never enjoyed walking in the woods, especially alone, and especially not in Africa. But right then, I saw a low hill, and I wanted to walk to the top of it. I felt drawn to go there, like it was calling to me.

Wandering slowly up the hill, I felt light and pleasant on my feet. After a few minutes, as I reached the crest of the hill, I heard my wife calling my name. The night air, the grassland, felt so good; I was reluctant to answer. I turned to see her standing at the bottom of the hill with two men from the tribe. She was waving her arms, yelling for me to come back. I didn't want to and tried to brush her off. But then I heard something in her voice, something that sounded like fear, like urgency. I could not ignore it. So, I walked back down the hill.

When I arrived at the bottom, the two men looked at me with shifting eyes. They were sweating, and so nervous they almost looked sickly. And then they told me why. At first, they found it a little strange that I had a desire to go walking by myself, especially after the ceremony. But they knew there was something significant about it, so they let me go, but kept close watch. As I made my way up the hill, they noticed that the grass along the side of my path was moving. It moved parallel with me and just a little behind. Right away, because they knew the land so well, including all its inhabitants—they knew what it was that caused the grass to move in such a way.

"It is a Hook Snake who called you to the hill," they said.

The Hook Snake owes its name to the great bone-like hooks at the end of its tail. They are part of the constrictor family and can grow up to thirty feet long. To hunt, they thrust their tail-hook forward, like a whip, latching into their prey and pulling them to the ground—before proceeding with the constriction part. As I walked so peacefully up the grassy hill, little did I know I had such an escort.

What I experienced in the ceremony was a great cleansing of old patterns, habits, limitations, connections, and experiences. The ceremony enhanced who I was, clearing the way, cleaning my spiritual domain—making way for a stronger connection to the divine.

After the ceremony, the healer informed the man that we were staying with, that if I had a dream that night, they should pay close attention because I was now like them—the dream may foretell of something to come. As he was telling this to our host, I watched from across the room. As they spoke, I witnessed the healer's head turn to the side, looking directly toward me, but at the same time, his head was still facing forward as he conversed with our host. He appeared to have, at that moment, two heads—one looked at me, the other at my friend. I realized he did this for a reason. He knew I was watching and he wanted to send a message, to assure me that indeed something unusual—something that changed me totally, had happened during the ceremony.

As predicted, I had a dream the night before we left. I shared this dream with our host in the morning, and he took it seriously, though I was not aware of his actions. He only listened and nodded silently as I relayed my vision to him. After listening with care to the dream, he made plans. Because of this dream, many lives were saved from a catastrophic event and the sequence of events that would have followed.

When I first decided to go to Africa, I decided it was for spiritual reasons. I could not foresee how strongly that decision would affect my journey. After this first trip to Africa, many things happened that changed me for good. I found that Africa listened—and very acutely. It heard my thoughts, my wishes, and my prayers even before I arrived.

A Degree with Prayers

Back in the states again, I enrolled at the university to get my master's degree in counseling. Going into the academic world again brought up great fear and anxiety. The lingering trauma of dyslexia and my challenges with learning had not completely dissolved. But I readied myself with fierce determination. Day and night, I devoted my time to studying, taking a double credit load so I would graduate as fast as possible. To avoid any confusion or mistakes, especially during tests, and because of the underlying fear of dyslexia, I decided I should memorize all the class materials—every word of every textbook. And so that is what I did. I studied for about ten hours per day, worked to save money, and did little else. It was not easy, but I had support, and in one year, I had completed everything—I was finally finished with my college education with close to three master's degrees: career counseling, school counseling; and I was one course away from a degree in city planning.

We were in the states for a little over one year before we went back to explore Africa.

The Pharaoh

Everywhere I looked while in Egypt, I saw the symbol of the eye. It was everywhere. I was reminded of the extraordinary vision I had before coming to Africa the first time, while driving across Iowa—the enormous eyeball staring down at me from the sky and the giant woman with wings. I found images of the Goddess called Isis everywhere. They looked strikingly like the female figure I saw in the vision.

The second night we were in Cairo, I could not sleep. The bed was too short and irritated my back, so I made a place for myself to stretch out on the floor. In the night, I awoke to a vibration all around me, as if the whole earth was trembling. A high-pitched sound accompanied the rumbling vibration. In the room was a short step near the bathroom door, and there in the dark, set upon the step sat a tiny man. He sat with his knees pulled up against his chest and his hands placed together beneath his chin, balled into fists. His skin had the texture of tough leather, and he wore a perfect brown suitcoat and pants. I could not take my eyes off him, but naturally, I was a little nervous, and I calculated just how far I had to run to reach the door.

Perhaps he was the spirit of someone who had stayed in this room previously, maybe someone who had passed away—just as I was combing through these (what seemed to me reasonable) thoughts, his eyes began to open. They opened, at first, into narrow slits. Bright light glowed from two thin lines between his eyelids. Slowly, he opened his eyes wider, and the light grew brighter. Then suddenly, his eyes flew wide open. A bright beam of light shot out from his eyes and struck my face. I felt a pressure against my head and a dizzying, nauseous feeling washed over me. When I gained my sight, I looked back toward the step where he sat. He was gone. Stunned, I was unable to sleep for the rest of the night.

The next day, we went around the city of Cairo, doing the usual tourist things. We visited a museum where a mummified person was on display in a glass case. As I approached the display, I noticed the leathery skin; the hands balled into fists, and legs pulled up against his chest. To my shock, I saw he was in the same position as the tiny figure who visited my room the previous night. On closer inspection, I found he was indeed the same person.

As soon as I saw him and recognized that he was a Pharaoh, the ill feeling that lingered since his visit disappeared in an instant.

Tiny Pyramids

We were eating at a restaurant that afternoon, when a man came through the door, looking all around the room, scanning the faces of the guests—he was searching for someone. As his eyes met mine, he headed straight toward our table.

"I have somewhere very special I think you should go," he said to me as he reached our table. He spoke as if we already knew each other.

At first, I was a little reluctant about his offer. There were many people, because we were tourists, who wanted to take us places— usually for money.

But then he said, "You really need to see this."

The way he said it, and the look in his eyes when he said it, gave me the impression that this was not an ordinary situation—and he was being sincere. So, I followed him. He was a cab driver, so we went to his car.

As we drove, he told me there were many places where Pharaohs were buried, and many of these places no one knew about. After we drove a while, he stopped the car, got out, and pointing, directed me toward what looked like an opening to a small path. He said he would wait for me there. Leaving him behind with the car, I followed his directions and soon came to a large, flat, open expanse. The sight I saw before me was mesmerizing. Spread across a wide, sand covered area, small pyramids, one after another, dotted the landscape. It looked like a pyramid city, only in miniature. Some of them were about five feet tall, some taller, fifteen to twenty feet. I had never heard of such a place—and in fact, it would be some time, decades, before anyone else knew of the existence of these small pyramids. There was a clear path to walk among the monuments, and I followed it.

As I walked, a gentle voice spoke to me. It told me many things about myself, about my life, and gave me many words of wisdom. I listened and walked through the landscape as if in a dream. I felt as if I was in another world completely.

The voice said: "There are many things people experience and many things that people will never understand, the Pharaohs here have ruled for a very long time. You will have challenges in your life, people will come to you and people may hurt you but you will help, and you will heal. Remember, the human condition will go on... and remember—you cannot change the human condition... remember that you will be just fine." This mysterious narrator said many other things as he educated me about the human condition and assured me about my place in the world. All throughout, he repeated that throughout my life I would be able to help others. As I walked, and as I listened, the most powerful feeling of gratitude came upon me.

Walking back the way I came, I found the taxi driver waiting. I did not know how much time had passed, but the sun was setting. Several hours must have gone by since I began my walk amongst the pyramids, yet it seemed not much time had passed at all, maybe only thirty minutes. I offered money to the driver who brought me there, but he refused.

"No, I cannot take your money," he said. "There are very few people who enter this place. You are here for a reason."

Later, reflecting upon this experience through meditation, I discovered that the taxi driver who sought me out that day was an ancient being, one who could transcend time and space. His work involves helping humankind. That day, he showed up to help me. So many moments in my life I have felt so honored—this was one of them.

Feet of Gold

Donkeys were to be our transport to the top of the hill. I really did not want to ride the poor animal for fear of damaging my back—or his. I told the tour guides I would jog up the hill instead, and meet them at the top. They looked at me like I was a little crazy. It was quite a long distance and a steep climb, not to mention the temperature and bright sun. I ignored them and started to run. I held onto a vision as I ran. I kept in my mind the feeling—as I climbed the hill—of the opposite; instead, I imagined myself moving at a swift pace downhill. As a young child, riding in the car with my aunt and my mother, I overheard their conversation. They spoke of going up the steep hill in the car and how more fuel was being consumed. Sitting in the back seat, the black vinyl sticking to my legs in the summer heat, I was interested in what they said, and I could feel my mind working. I told them my idea.

"Imagine you are going downhill instead of uphill, that way you can save on gas!" I believed my discovery could help them to save money, which was the topic they seemed rather concerned over.

Well, I can't say that the adults in this situation took me too seriously, but they also did not put me down. My aunt nodded, glancing back at me through the rearview mirror, her warm brown eyes letting me know she heard me. She agreed to try it.

As I ran up the steep hill that day, I noticed the running motion became smooth and effortless as I held onto the downhill way of visualization. I met the party at the top, the noontime sun blazing. I was not out of breath and had no sweat on my body. The group eyed me with a little suspicion. Some were curious, but no one said a word.

After a time in Cairo, we visited a city called Luxor. A small hotel sat just off the main street, painted green with a wide front porch. Guests sat out front chatting in the evening hours, while small dogs and pigs, sometimes monkeys, wrestled in the street. Somehow (minus the monkeys), it reminded me of my hometown in Iowa.

That night, once again, I slept on the floor. I was half asleep when I heard the same strange high-pitched sound that I had heard in Cairo. I tried to move my body but found I could not. It was as if some tremendous force had pinned me to the ground. I could only turn my head a fraction to one side.

From my view on the floor, I saw a pair of feet moving toward me. These were no ordinary feet. They looked human but made of golden light. Bright beams and flashing sparks were shooting from them in all directions. Then I heard a booming voice.

"You need to look at my face," it said.

I tried with all the strength of my will to move my head so I could see his face. Still, I could not.

"You must look upon my face," it repeated. "If you don't, I will have to leave… or you will die."

I tried and tried again to move my muscles, but I was locked in place.

After a pause, the voice said, "I must go. Don't worry, you will be ok." I watched, helpless as the golden feet turned away from me and disappeared.

The next day, I awoke and was sick beyond words. My energy was so weak, I could not stand. And I began to lose weight at an alarming rate. It felt like the mass of my body was melting away, my material form disintegrating by the minute. I was too weak to get up to go anywhere, so a doctor came to see me and gave me medicine, but nothing seemed to have an effect and my weight kept dropping.

After twenty-four hours, I had lost over thirty pounds. I looked in the mirror and hardly knew my image. The doctor decided that it was too serious. I needed to return to the US to seek medical treatment right away. All while this was happening, I kept thinking about the sparkling golden feet, and hearing the words the voice had said to me—*not to worry, I would be ok.*

Plans were being made for our emergency departure. That morning, I felt an urgent need for fresh air. I was too weak to walk, and no wheelchair was available, so two men carried me in a wooden chair and set me on the front porch. As I sat there, taking long breaths of air, I heard a beautiful melody coming from a vendor's stand across the street. It sounded like chanting. I told my friends that I would like to go closer to the music. It seemed important—I needed to listen and be near to it. So, once again, they lifted me, along with the chair. As I sat beside the vendor's cart and listened, drifting in and out of consciousness, I entered into a state of soft dreaming. The beautiful chanting songs lulled my mind and brought peace to my body, to my whole being.

After listening for a while, fading in and out, I began to feel much better. Suddenly, I opened my eyes wide and straightened up in my chair. I was awake and rejuvenated. I asked the vendor, who looked a little perplexed, if I could purchase a copy of the recording. Then, I stood up from the seat they had carried me on, paid the man for the tape, took my chair and walked back to the hotel, as if nothing ever happened—as if I was in complete health.

Everyone—my wife, the doctor, the friends who were helping—were in shock when they saw me walk through the door carrying my chair. Just moments earlier, it was questionable whether I might die. They didn't know if they could really trust their eyes. So, before canceling the recently adjusted travel plans to return to the states, we decided to wait at least a day.

Many years later, back in the states, I relayed this story to some young Muslim friends. They had an immediate excited reaction.

"It's the Qur'an!" They exclaimed, beaming with smiles.

They were certain that it was the power of the prayer music that helped me to heal. They had heard many miraculous stories that occurred because of listening to the chanting of these sacred words.

Moses

The next day, I felt my vitality had returned, and had no desire to leave Africa. I was ready to continue with our travels. Somehow, I convinced the others that I was back to normal and to stop worrying. Many unusual things had happened while in Africa, so there was a degree of flexibility and acceptance for unexplainable phenomena. That afternoon, we went to visit the famous Mount Sinai—a name I heard many times throughout life in relation to the Bible. I decided I wanted to run up the steep road that led to the top of the mountain, just as I had before, on another climb—using the visualizing technique of imagining I was running downhill instead of up.

To begin the climb, I first had to pass through a Greek Orthodox cathedral at the base of the mountain. As I made my way through the long columns and archways of the church, I saw a group of robed clergymen headed in my direction. They walked in a regimental-like procession, with one priest leading the way out front, while other holy men in robes flanked behind, side by side, two by two. I noticed that the man in the front had been staring at me for some time. The whole procession marched across the courtyard and stopped just in front of me.

The priest, who was in the lead, stepped forward, getting close to my face, meeting me eye to eye.

"My goodness," he said, looking me up and down, "you look just like Moses... just like him!"

With a glimmer in his eye, he looked me over for several moments. Then he went on his way, the procession of robes in his wake, the soft bustling sound of fabric.

I was surprised—I never would have thought that Moses looked anything like me.

Upon reaching the top of the Mount Sinai, I found only one other man. He was sitting on a large, flat stone. I said hello, but realized he did not speak English, so I made gestures with my hands to let him know I would like to sit as well. He understood and pointed me toward another large, flat stone. As I sat there, I fell into a deep, relaxed state. I lay back upon the stone. With my eyes closed, geometric shapes and patterns appeared on the screen of my vision. Each formation was half red and half white. They appeared and disappeared, moving in and out, changing formation consistently. I fell into the trance of the repeated patterns and was no longer conscious of the world around me. When I awoke, the other man was gone. I gazed upon the flat stone where he sat and had a strong feeling of comfort and contentment—I did not want to leave.

Jinga's Place in the Bowl

The day I met Mamadou was destined to be. At the train station, we were about to leave the area and go on to another city, when we noticed a couple walking toward us. It was late at night and there were not many other people around. They had a striking appearance. The man had dark brown skin and was dressed in a fine grey suit. The woman had very pale skin, almost ivory, and looked like she came from northern Europe. Coming from opposite directions, we approached the ticket window at the same time. The couple politely gestured for us to go ahead of them, and we struck up a conversation. It turned out that this man, Mamadou, was a serious martial artist. He competed worldwide in karate and at a high level. His fiancé, the slender blonde woman standing at his side, was from Sweden. I told him a little about my experiences with Kung Fu, and he was eager to talk more.

He was curious to know why we were in Senegal and what we wanted to do. I told him I wanted to meet with spiritual people, and we also wanted to experience the culture and eat good food. His face lit up with delight. He said that we must go to meet his mother. She knew many healers and spiritual people. Also, she made the best food in the area.

"Please, stay for a couple of days here with my family," he urged.

So, we took a cab that night to Mamadou's mother's house.

Two large wooden gates led into a spacious courtyard surrounded on three sides by a large concrete house with many doors and windows. Mamadou's family stayed in the rooms surrounding the courtyard—his sisters and brothers with their husbands and wives. There was also room for the occasional guest, like us. Mamadou led us to our room and pointed to where he and his fiancé stayed at the far end of the long pavilion.

The next morning, we met the matriarch of the house. Mamadou's mother was someone extraordinary. When she looked at you, it seemed she looked right through you. Her face looked as if she were wearing a mask. I have never seen another face like it. When her eyes moved—they moved as if they were behind something, behind the mask of her still face—and those eyes could see more than the average person. She called me Jinga.

"No, it's Jim," I tried to correct her.

"No!" she would reply adamantly, "Jinga!"

"There is some reason she calls you this," explained Mamadou. "She knows your name and knows how to say it, yet she insists—it's Jinga."

I never knew what this name meant to her. But, as she introduced me to others as Jinga, they would *hmmm* and nod their heads, examining me with their thoughts, as if they knew exactly what she meant by the name.

During the daytime, I often spent time with Mamadou's little brother. He was only eight years old. We played silly games and made faces and laughed with each other. His mother's watchful eyes were always nearby. I could tell, though, that she liked me—she approved. And that was important because she was at the head of the household and a very strong and respected woman.

At mealtime in the house, all the men gathered in the main room around a low table. One great bowl of food sat in the middle. It always amazed me at how everyone knew exactly where in the bowl to eat their portion. It was as if there were invisible lines drawn in the food—the portions divided perfectly according to however many people were there at the table. I asked Mamadou about this one day.

"How do you know where in the bowl to eat?" I asked.

"You just eat the portion that is right in front of you!" He replied, laughing a little.

The locals had a way of jesting about people who were outsiders: "They do not know their place in the bowl."

African Martial Arts

Moving through the air like cats flying, like shifting smoke in the wind; dark, fluid shapes twisted and darted across the sky, soft and cutting. They remained above the ground for several moments at a time—dancing, sharp silhouettes. It seemed they hardly touched the ground. And when they did, their feet only grazed the surface before lifting off again.

I was witnessing the beauty of African martial art style.

Mamadou and I had many long conversations, sometimes stretching from nighttime into the early reaches of morning. He was passionate about the study of martial arts, and our talks often went in that direction. I told him about my past, practicing Kung-Fu. He listened closely as I relayed stories about experiencing time moving in slow motion—how I could see my opponent's moves before they moved. Mamadou had heard of this technique before. In the martial arts world, there were always many stories in circulation. He was eager to know more.

"You should become our teacher," he said with gravity.

"No, no." I shook my head. "I have not practiced for many years. I gave it up for a reason."

What I saw that night as they sparred was the most beautiful display of martial arts I have ever seen. That night, they were my teachers.

A Place out of No Place

One morning, Mamadou took us into town, to the marketplace. It was a lively scene, full of the smells of spices and food, and sounds of people bustling about, preparing for the day. There was conversation, laughter, kids and animals; smoke and steam from nearby kitchens trailing through the street.

"See that man, he is a medicine man, and that woman over there, she makes herbal treatments," Mamadou directed our attention to the people of the town. "And this man here is a historian. He knows the names of everyone who has ever been through this town."

As we strolled down the main street, the vibrant style, the smells, and the sounds washed through me like music.

"Do you want to meet someone special?" Mamadou asked.

"Yes, of course," I said.

"I have someone," he said.

"Is there something you need to do first to get in touch?" I asked.

"I just did," he replied, smiling. Nothing had happened; nothing that we could see anyway.

We walked down a busy street until we stopped in front of a fence made completely of what looked like driftwood. All the pieces were smooth and slightly rounded. On closer inspection, I noticed they wove together, like pieces of a puzzle. Each piece fit each other with precision.

When we entered through the ornate wooden gate, we encountered a scene that looked like something from Japan—like a sculptural garden. A small yard of perfectly raked sand formed patterned lines, with larger stones placed decoratively within, forming an image of islands within waves. An elevated wooden walkway, also made of narrow driftwood-like pieces, led to the front porch of a humble but tidy house. The double doors stood wide open and inside a sparse room, busy behind a low desk, a man sat writing with a pencil. Wearing a blue silk outfit, his skin was deep ebony brown, and his features were sharp.

"Hello", he said.

I noticed he spoke English perfectly, and with no accent.

As if he could hear my thoughts, he said: "I speak many languages."

He proceeded to tell us several things about ourselves.

"How is it you know so much about us when we only just met?" I asked.

"Mamadou has a way to get in touch with me when he needs to," was all he said. "How can I help you?"

I told him I was interested in spirituality. He nodded as if he expected that.

First, he addressed my wife and told her about what was going to happen, in general, while she was in Africa. He also told her she would return to the USA, while her husband (me) would stay in Africa. Then he held out a pencil, the tip facing upward.

"Think about what you want and blow on the tip of the pencil three times," he instructed her.

She did this, and then he took the pencil and began drawing lines on a page. As he made the marks, he told her all about herself and her life, past and future.

Then it was my turn. I blew on the pencil. He made more lines. He said many things about my life. Here, I will only mention a few:

"You have been in front of many people... many people shouting your name. While you are in Africa, you will find what you are looking for. This trip is very important. One day, you will come back. We may see each other again."

As he spoke, I found it difficult to hear him. His voice sounded like it had an echo—the sound bouncing and ricocheting through some cavernous space.

"Can I do what you do with the pencil?" I asked him.

"Of course," he replied, "before you leave, you will know how to do this."

The next day, I could remember nothing about this encounter and could not think of anything this mysterious man had said to me. It was as if parts of my memory were erased. I told Mamadou about my dilemma. He agreed we should go back to find this man again. But when we got to the place where the house sat, it was no longer there. There was not even a space where it could have been. The same buildings that sat on either side of his house the day before were there, exactly as they were before, except now, there was no space in between them—the space his house would have occupied. No fence, no sand, no porch—nothing. No space existed where his house could have possibly been placed. It was as if he created a space out of no space; as if a pocket in the atmosphere had unzipped only for a moment, and there he was.

Mamadou shrugged and said, "Well, I guess he is not here. Sometimes it's like this." We walked away. "You will probably never see him again. This can mean that there may be a lesson you need to learn first."

We decided to leave Senegal and continue traveling, first to Mali— Mamadou would accompany us there. I had a feeling, though, that my time was not over with the people and the land in Senegal. There was more waiting. As we drove away with Mamadou, I knew I would be back.

Sound and Light

As soon as we got into Mali, I heard music everywhere, except no one was playing any instrument, nor was there any recording or speakers playing any sound. No one around me could hear any music. Only I could hear it. Everywhere I went, and at all times, beautifully strange melodies were playing, like a private soundtrack, along to my every movement. While I walked down the street, while I observed the scenery, the people, the animals—the music kept its rhythm and melody going. The sound and style were nothing familiar to me, but beautiful. It was full of life and energy, and at the same time, not intrusive at all. It went along with my day and my actions seamlessly. While this was happening, I noticed I was unable to have any kind of internal dialog, like when I was a child. Nothing—no thoughts, no memories, no judgement—I was only there, observing the world around me. None of the usual ramble that goes on in the mind. Any kind of expression realized within was in the moment, and never lingered.

The music that accompanied me was like a living being. It had its own way of communication. It was like a friend. For instance, when I walked down the street and came to an intersection; I looked to the left, but when I looked right, the music became louder. So, I took that as my cue, that was the way to go, and I turned right.

The sound became like a guide, and we were having a constant conversation.

I did not get much sleep because when I closed my eyes, accompanying the music, a brilliant show of geometric shapes and animated, bright, and colorful lines would appear behind my eyes. The designs moved to the music, continually shifting and merging, fading away, and then drawing back together again like a dance. Constantly being created, and constantly dissolving into other forms. To my amazement, this bizarre experience kept its pace, day and night, for the entire three weeks I was in Mali.

After a little more traveling, I felt a pull to go back to Senegal and to Mamadou's house. There was something waiting for me, though I did not know what. My wife decided to go a separate direction and then back to the US. I would meet her there later, after I had more time in Senegal. The man who made lines with the pencil, who predicted our future, was correct—she would leave, and I would stay.

Back in Senegal, I met with more people who could see my future and knew my life. Several of them traveled great distances to help me spiritually, and some of them were very old people. They could be called ancients, or immortals. They were much older than I thought was possible for humans—I believe, after hearing stories from locals, that they were near six hundred years old. I am not permitted to tell some of these stories at this time, but I am forever grateful to the beautiful and powerful beings who helped me to carve a life path. After meeting with these ancient people, and the experiences which followed, it was as if a throughway became available to me; I was able to encounter the people and situations that I needed to usher me into the way that was best.

I have never felt as welcome in any place as I did in Africa. Whether people had very little, or plenty—the words *you are welcome* meant something. Wherever I went, when African people addressed me, they looked me in the eye, and they spoke to my humanity at its center. They always recognized me as a fellow human being, deserving of respect. I felt embraced consistently by some great force—a protective embrace from something ancient, something much greater than myself.

With these words, I wish to not only share these stories with you, dear reader, about Africa, but to convey the love and the warm welcome I received. My time on this continent included some of the best moments of my life. My feet were firmly planted on the ground. It was the only time I have ever experienced such a strong feeling of family—a family who would bring you into their arms time and time again, no matter what.

All the time I was there, it seemed that people knew the reason I was there more than I did. They knew I had come to heal my spirit, as if it was written. Several medicine people had a similar message for me. They could *see* me. They could see what I was meant to be in this world. These people and this land were helping me to reconnect to a vibration that would help me put the pieces of my life together, so that I may become who I needed to be spiritually. To find home. To find my purpose. Sometimes I wonder if I might wake up and find myself still there, in Africa—and all the time which followed will have only been a dream.

Upon returning to the states, we started saving money again, living in North Carolina, and briefly in Texas. We planned for another trip. Next, it would be to India, but first I had to say goodbye to two of the most important figures in my life.

Clear Water

I will not forget the look on my father's face the day I played the harmonica for him. We were at his house in Cedar Rapids. It was not long after I had first moved to Minnesota, and I was visiting, on a break from teaching kids in school. As I played, he closed his eyes, tilted his head back into his chair, and a smile came across his face like he found a spot of heaven. I played in one room while he rocked his chair in the other. During this visit, before our first trip to Africa, my father told me about the cancer. He didn't have long.

Playing the blues harp was, I'm sure, nothing my father expected from me. I was a rather quiet and shy kid. As a lover of music, all he could do was enjoy the moment and sit back with a grin. Later, I realized the weight of that moment, and how much it meant to him. Most of his life, he worked in the stockyard and as a butcher. He took care of family and helped in the community, but never got to go to college himself. Something he would have loved to do. Now, his son—with a degree and a career—was playing the blues harmonica in his living room. It meant a great deal of peace for him. Now, it meant I would be ok in the world. He no longer had to worry.

A year or so later, after returning from our second trip to Africa, I went to visit the Healer in Boston. I sat in his room, and we chatted like usual as I soaked my feet in something he called "the blue medicine."

About an hour passed by, as my feet sat in a tub filled with bright blue liquid—when the Healer paused and then said, "That's it, lad. You're done."

I looked down at my feet to find the liquid had turned completely clear—clear as water. Usually, after soaking, the water was blue, and my feet, after taking them out of the tub, held a slight blue tint.

"No need to come back," he said. "You're done."

It had been thirteen years since we first met. The Healer became a strong part of my life, someone I looked to. Each year, as I went to spend time with him, I witnessed a man full of compassion and dedicated to helping others.

Many times, as I sat with him in his room, he'd say, "Lad, you'll see—one day you'll do even more than me."

It was difficult for me to take him too seriously.

"You'll change the way people think... many, many people." His enthusiasm was robust.

I was young, and mostly I couldn't bring myself to believe him when he said these things about me. I brushed his words aside like they were merely a compliment—something to boost my spirit, to make me feel good. But the Healer knew and saw more than the average person. He knew about my future; and knew I was on a path toward healing work and service long before I did. I was fortunate to be in his company. He played a significant role in who I am today.

Two months later, as I was sleeping, the Healer came to me in a vision. He woke me from slumber, embraced me with gusto, and then flew off in a burst of light. A little while later, I received the news that he had passed away.

Only a few weeks after that, I got a phone call—my father was in his last days. I traveled west to say goodbye.

Some say that music is something from the heavens. That each note released to the universe sails on and on—into infinity. The love I received from my father in the time we had together was enough to carry me through life. Even though the time we had was short—the love was so strong. It was lasting. I had experienced being separated from him before. And as I said goodbye for the last time, I knew that even though he would no longer be physically present in this world, his love was always there—it would go on and on.

Two important men were gone from my life; two men who were a constant current of strength and support behind me. Knowing they were there, helped me along. My father, in his steadfast loyalty and love; I knew I could go to him if ever I needed. And the Healer with his wild ways of knowing and communicating on a spiritual, a heart level, gave me an example of healing and unconditional love toward others. Through the consistent, invaluable love and respect from these men, I was able to find myself and find my place of stability in the world. Now, a page had turned. Although I knew part of them would always be with me, on a spiritual level—it was time for me to continue down my path without them.

After living in the US a bit and saving more money, we set off to travel to distant, ancient lands, once again.

Famous in India

It was 1987. After getting a cab upon arriving in India, I noticed the driver's eyes in his rear-view mirror. He was constantly glancing back at me. I thought: *Maybe this is normal. I don't know the culture.* Being an experienced traveler, I was accustomed to not knowing, and ready to accept many things unknown.

"Sir, you look very much like a very famous cricket player." The driver said in a serious tone.

"Really?" I replied, although I wasn't all that interested. I thought there were probably many athletes who shared similar features.

"You should be careful," he continued.

That statement caught my attention—*why should I be careful? I thought. Maybe this is something he says to every foreigner.* I shrugged it off, and we went about our day, eventually forgetting all about it.

Later, while we were out, someone gestured to me and then made a motion with their arms, like they were moving a cricket bat through the air. I shook my head, smiling, and made a gesture in return, lifting my arms forward like I was shooting a basketball into the hoop. They shook their head, and with a sly smile (like they knew what I was up to and were in on the secret) they repeated the batting gesture.

What was this? I thought, perplexed.

This same scenario, with the cricket-batting motion, repeated several times throughout the day, from different people, in different parts of the city. I began to think that there may be something more to what the cab driver said.

Things became stranger when, in the evening, we went to see a movie at the theater. While standing in line for a ticket, with many people ahead of us, someone suddenly grabbed my arm, dragging me up to the front of the line. Even though I did not understand what he was saying, I could tell by the rhythm and tone of his language, he was excited about something. As we reached the head of the line, I saw the ticket clerk's eyes grow wide after glancing at me. A few serious words were exchanged between the two men, and then we were hustled through, into the empty theater, and quickly seated, before anyone else.

We were having quite a good time, believing that because we were tourists, or maybe because we looked different from most people around us, we were being treated with the highest quality of service. We laughed and smiled, full of gratitude, and enjoyed the special treatment. In a little time after we were seated, the man who had pulled us from the line brought us food, sweet snacks and drinks— everything one could want from an Indian movie house. We had no choice but to sit and smile and go along with it. As the movie played, people in the theater were pointing and staring at us. They were watching us more than the film. I realized then that we may be facing a serious dilemma: apparently, I was being mistaken for someone hugely famous. All of these people thought I was someone else—but I did not know who.

That evening, we went to a popular and crowded area in the city. For some reason, we thought that was the safe thing to do. As we were walking down the street, we heard someone yell. I turned to see what the commotion was and spotted a man pointing and running. I glanced around trying to spot what he was pointing to—when I realized he was pointing in our direction. As he ran, he was shouting something, and several other people joined him. In moments, there was a small crowd breaking into a run, heading straight toward us. We stood there like scared animals in the middle of the road. Before we knew what to do, there were about fifty people surrounding us, with sounds of excitement, reaching out and trying to touch me. Because I was taller than most, I could look around over the tops of heads to see the entire street. What I saw terrified me—crowds of people, streets full, were running toward us—more and more were joining in the rush. Within minutes, a mob had surrounded us. It was becoming dangerous, not just for us, but for everyone there. We did not want a stampede. Then, I spotted a car. It was honking its horn with ferocity, creeping its way through the crowd. When it reached us, the driver swung the door open.

"Get in! Get in!" He yelled.

We barely squeezed inside, and as we shut the door, a throng of people enveloped the car, leaving hands and faces pressing against the windows. We were stunned.

"What are you doing here?" the cab driver was nearly shouting, "You should know better!" He admonished us.

"Wait a minute," I said, "I am not who you think I am. I'm an American and I do not play cricket!"

I had to repeat myself several times because he did not believe me. The driver kept shaking his head in disbelief as I tried to convince him. Finally, he relented.

"This cannot be!" He exclaimed. "You could be his twin!"

Over a prolonged pause, in which the cab driver seemed to be processing the information, trying to work out what should happen next, all he could say was, "Oh! This is really not good..."

After the incident with the mob, we had to be careful wherever we went. We always took a cab and never went anywhere that was too popular. But even then, people would pull me aside, sometimes offering small gifts. When we ate at restaurants, usually the meals were free. Even when I told them I did not play cricket; I was not who they thought I was—they didn't believe me; they thought I was only trying to hide my identity. They would always shake their heads, smiling graciously, and make the motion—one that was becoming very familiar—like they were going up to bat.

Only recently, I found out who they thought I was—he was part of the East Indies team and one of the most famous cricket players of all time. He was so famous that he was granted knighthood. When I found his image, I saw it was true—we shared a significant resemblance to one another.

The Floating Man

When we first came upon the man who was floating in the air, we had been strolling around a small village in southern India, enjoying a relaxed day. The street was bustling with the usual day-to-day events—kids running down the alley, the occasional cow plodding by, women with their armloads of fabric, or carrying bulbous baskets upon their heads. And then there he was. The man floated in the air about twenty feet above it all. He was lying horizontally, and looked just as he would if he were lying in a bed. When my wife saw him, she froze in place, at a loss for words, her eyes fixed upon his still form. After our travels in Africa, and witnessing so many unusual things—we knew anything was possible. Of course, this was a little extraordinary. He was only a few yards away. No one on the busy street around us paid him any mind.

"I'm going to go over and check this out," I said.

I walked over until I was standing just below where he was hovering and looked up at him. He was sleeping and seemed quite comfortable. I could hear his heavy breathing. The strangest thing was, at that moment, everything felt completely normal to me. It felt the same as if I were looking at a man who was napping on a park bench. Yet here I was—standing beneath a man who was floating in the air next to a small tree. There was not much more to it, and after a few minutes, we went on our way.

Many big changes awaited us back in the states.

Keepin'-It-Together-Nance

After our travels, my wife and I decided to separate. She had her PhD. and was focused on her career. While I went back to Minnesota, where I had many connections within the school district from the time I had worked there years before.

It was good to be back with the kids—always a worthwhile focus. In my spare time, I continued to explore spirituality, and was still committed to searching for a Qigong Master. After a couple of years of working in the school district, I became friends with a school principal. He was an indigenous person and part of the Ojibwe tribal community. We often would sit and chat, telling stories, and talking about spiritual matters. One day, he invited me to take part in a sweat lodge ceremony. He had built a lodge on his property in the countryside and was hosting the event regularly. He told me to come. Before the ceremony, his task was to collect and prepare the wood. This was something he did before each event. I told him I would come and help him gather the wood.

The sweat-lodge was a low, dome shaped structure. Entering through the short opening, I had to bend at the waist, stooping low to the ground. Red-hot stones were placed inside, in the middle of the circle. Community members, elders, and medicine people sat together around the center as the air became hot and sweat began to form. We sat for cleansing, for prayer, and for health.

One day, before another type of ceremony, after going out into the woods and returning with a pile of kindling in my arms, I noticed several members of the group watching me.

"Nance," one of them called out, "do you know there are two of you?"

I thought, at first, my friends were joking. I was accustomed to their unique style of humor.

"We saw you walk into the forest, and then we saw another one of you. The other one of you split off and walked in that direction," he continued, pointing in the direction one of me went. "On your way back, there were two of you, but then one of you disappeared and sank into the ground."

As they described the story in detail, I could see they were not joking about what they had witnessed. A brief silence followed. I didn't know how to respond.

"From now on, we'll call you Keepin'-It-Together-Nance." Everyone had a laugh then. Even though they were serious, there was always room for humor.

Apparently, my role as wood-gatherer for the sweat lodge carried more significance than I knew. After two years of gathering wood, my friend, the principal, told me that the elders wanted to know if there was something I wanted in return for my service.

"No, thank you," I said. "It was enough to take part in these ceremonies. I do not need more."

But the elders persisted. They knew there was something more. They felt there was a reason I was there.

"Find what it is you are looking for, and we may be able to help you," my friend said.

And then one day it came to me. There was something I had been searching for. I called my friend right away.

"I know what it is," I said. "I know what I want—what I've been searching for."

"Ok," he said, "but don't tell me what it is. Just keep it to yourself and come to the lodge."

I was told to come on a particular day. There, a special ceremony was arranged just for me. There was prayer, and song, smoke, and drums. My friend instructed me on how to concentrate, how to pray. My request, which I kept inside my heart, was that I would finally find what I had been searching for all these years—a spiritual teacher, a Qigong Master.

The Call

The adventures I had been on, the people I met, the events—sometimes bizarre, sometimes magical—left me churning with questions, and fervent in my pursuit of finding answers.

It was 1992, and I had been living and working in the city of Minneapolis for several years. The city had given me so much, yet I felt that our time together was ending. Right from the beginning, the city opened its arms to me, letting me know I would be taken care of. The first few days after I arrived, I went to a health food grocery store. It was a small place, not far from where I was staying. When my friend and I arrived, they were just closing. A woman on the other side of the glass front door was busy flipping around the sign as we walked up. But she unlocked the door when she saw us.

Opening it by a crack, she said, "Wait right here. I have something for you."

I thought she must be mistaking me for someone else. Watching her through the window, I saw her run around the store, filling two paper bags with food and groceries. In a few minutes, she was back.

"Here you go, enjoy." She said, smiling, placing the full grocery bags into our arms.

Next, for several weeks, I found money on the ground every day. These were my first experiences in Minneapolis. Now, here I was, almost fifteen years later, about to say goodbye. The words of my father haunted me: *Son, never leave that town. Something good is waiting for you.*

Although I enjoyed working with the kids, something was missing. I was still searching for something that would fulfill me spiritually. A friend in Arizona I had known since I was a child, told me there was community work for me there if I wanted. Also, there were rumors of a Qigong Master in the vicinity. So, I decided to leave Minneapolis, the town that had embraced and nourished me. I quit my job, had my bags packed and was ready to go within a week, when I received a phone call from a friend.

"I thought you might like to know," she said, "a Qigong Master will be coming to Minneapolis from China in one year—his name is Chunyi Lin."

Part II
The Way

When I was a child, someone said to me—if I could ask a question, any question, in the right way, no matter what, the answer would eventually come. Throughout my life, I have found this to be true. The answers came to me, not always through words, but often through sensations. I began to pay attention and recognize the different sensations and feelings. Sometimes, I could tell when I met someone, before they spoke a word, that they were asking particular questions about life. In this way, I would quietly investigate and observe the world.

There was a kind of knowing that helped me understand there was more to life than having material things, more than human connections or worldly affairs. I started to look at the trees, the ground, the world around me, in a different manner. Many things can inform you, talk to you, even answer questions. From an early age, the healing energy of life was preparing me for what was to be. The reality of this conversation— this instruction and guidance, as a presence in my life—became very real. I have found that this relationship never goes away.

The Arrival

Records dating back more than seven thousand years, reveal the science and practice of Qigong in China. Taoist Masters studied the natural world: animals, plants, weather, stars, and the human body, to name a few, as well as subtler forms of energy—the energy and intelligence behind life itself. *What tells your heart when and how to beat? What tells your hair to grow?* Qigong is the study of life. It is the study of the intelligent energy that is constantly at work, moving and transforming within all things.

As a young kid at church, I would often hear about how God could heal people through something called miracles. Often, people in the church prayed for miracles for those who were ill. I couldn't help but wonder, *why are people getting sick and going to the hospital if God can heal?* I thought about it often. Other questions ran through my young mind. *Why can't the loneliness of people be cured? Why is there war?* When I found no one had the answers to my questions, eventually, instead of asking others, I began to ask within.

These questions grew into something like a prayer. Small events changed me, and I gradually became a person who could listen in a different way. I could look at a point on a blank wall and feel something coming back at me. Sometimes wandering around my neighborhood when I was a boy, I'd feel sensations and emotions coming from the houses. I was asking, even then, similar questions that others have asked since ancient times—questions that led them to seek answers, questions that may have led to something like Qigong.

Twenty-seven years had passed since the Kung Fu Master told me to stop martial arts training and to seek a Qigong Master. After I received the news of Master Lin's pending arrival in Minnesota, I canceled my travel plans immediately, re-established some part time work, and waited.

Reflections with a Master

Our reason, our purpose for being here, goes far beyond what we can clearly see.

I received the phone call from Esther in 1994, in Minneapolis. She informed me that Master Lin had arrived from China and was in town, ready to see me. I headed over to the house where he was staying. It had been one year since I first heard his name.

Master Lin was in one chair, I in the other as we sat in Esther's living room facing one another. Mirrors ran the length of the room on each side, covering the walls behind us. So, as I sat facing Master Lin, I saw thousands of repeated images of him, and thousands of myself on either side. Our reflected images in the mirrors joined in a symmetrical arc and went on into infinity.

In the room of mirrors, as I sat across from Master Lin, he worked with my energy (qi), using Qigong techniques taught to him by Masters in China. Moving his hands around lightly, standing near, but not touching, he told me to close my eyes and to relax.

Years of playing high impact sports left me with many long-term injuries and resulted in some serious and enduring damage to my body. Even though I was not yet at an old age, it was difficult for me to remain upright for very long. I could only stand for a few hours at a time during the day. Also, after injuring my shoulders—I could not raise my arms past shoulder-height. The upper cabinets in my kitchen were always completely bare because everything had to be placed on the lower shelves, so I could reach without extending too far. Walking was hard because of spinal damage and several surgeries, as well as old injuries to my ankles and knees. In my day-to-day life, somehow, through small and not so small miracles, I could get through the workday and do what I needed to, but it was not easy.

After about twenty minutes, when Master Lin finished with the healing work, he simply told me he had helped to remove the blockages. I got up to leave, not noticing much difference at first (I was still buzzing on account that I had finally met a Qigong Master) but as I walked the short distance to my car, and then bent down to get into the driver's seat, I noticed the absence of the usual discomfort. Normally, bending down to do anything, partly because I am six-and-a-half feet tall, and because of the pain of old injuries—to get into the seat of my car was an awkward challenge. This time, though, the usual aches were not there. Then, when I arrived at home, out of curiosity, even though it was normally impossible, I tried raising my arms. They went up and up, and to my amazement, went almost all the way straight up above my head. I hadn't been able to do that in many years. Over the next couple of days after the healing session, the changes in my body and in my mobility became apparent. Around eighty percent of my mobility was restored after that first session with Master Lin. It was then that I knew, this Qigong Master, Master Chunyi Lin, was the one I had been searching for. I decided with firm determination—I would do whatever I needed to do to learn from him.

From that day forward, if Master Lin gave a lecture—I was there. If he taught a class—I was there. I went to every talk, every gathering, and each class. It seemed that I saw him everywhere I went. Once, I was in a parking lot, about to turn into a parking space, when I noticed another car was trying to park in the same space. I looked up at the driver, astounded to find that it was Master Lin. So, this is how it began. Qigong became my complete vision.

When it comes to Qigong, the deeper into it you get, the depth of Qigong comes to you. It awakens in you a perspective, and the ability to integrate that perspective into your life and into your practice.

Soon, I was helping to carry Qigong books and materials to Master Lin's classes. I sat in the back of the room, listening, watching. After, I helped distribute books to students. I witnessed as the classes started out with just a few people in a living room, and in less than two years, classes had grown to about eighty people. It was around this time that Spring Forest Qigong was born.

When I first began learning from Master Lin, I still did not really know what Qigong was about. The words of the Kung Fu Master, and the mysteries behind experiences in my life kept questions streaming through my mind. When the Kung Fu Master told me I needed to find someone to teach me Qigong, I believed I would find the answers I was looking for. Yet, through all this time, I thought Qigong was related to martial arts, and that by studying Qigong, I would continue to study martial arts, but perhaps a different style. Instead, what I discovered was a powerful healing art beyond anything I could have imagined.

Spring Forest Qigong is the art and practice in studying intelligent energy (qi) and learning how to cultivate this energy to help the body, mind, and spirit heal at all levels. Master Lin has created a practice system based on ancient knowledge passed down from Masters in China involving gentle movement, meditation, sound, and breath. It is so simple, yet so effective. Beginner students of Spring Forest Qigong, right away, can help themselves not only to heal faster, but also learn the ability to help others to heal.

My goal, at first, was to learn as much as I could. I had waited so long to find Qigong. Also, my goal was to support Master Lin as much, and in any way that I could. I was committed for the long term. I accompanied Master Lin around the Midwest as he taught classes and lectured; all the while I learned more and more.

My life had been preparing me all along.

Healing

If you want to understand about life as an energetic being, you need to understand that life has been trying to teach us about who we are. The gift of Qigong is that we begin to know more about who we are from an energetic perspective.

After about a year and a half of attending the classes and practicing Qigong, Chunyi suggested that I should do healing work. At first, I was a little surprised. I had not imagined myself as a healer. But, I went ahead and put the word out in the community: if there was anyone who could use help with their health, let me know, I would do my best.

I began to receive some calls. All the people who called me then, seven of them, were in critical health conditions. Several could not move from their beds. So, I began a routine to visit them regularly where they lived. I worked with their energy—clearing energy channels, removing blockages—using the skills I had learned through Spring Forest Qigong. Often, we spent time sitting and talking, enjoying quiet moments, sharing stories from our lives. They were all such beautiful people, and with all my heart I wished to help them.

One week, I didn't receive a call from one of these people. I learned they had passed away. Another week, someone else was gone. One by one, they all moved on from this life. I felt so sad and discouraged about this. Wanting to help them so badly, I began to doubt if I had what it took to be a healer. I went to consult Master Lin and told him what had happened.

"Each person was so incredible. They had so much peace, like angels, yet I wasn't able to save them. Should I be doing this?" I asked.

He told me not to spend too much time worrying, and to just keep practicing. So, I did. I kept practicing every day. I was determined to do better. Then, more people started coming to me, asking for healing. I would always do my best to help them. I noticed some people I was working with started feeling better, and other times, they came back. They told others, and more and more people started showing up at my door, requesting my help. There were days, returning home from work, I found a line of people waiting outside my front door. Around this time, Spring Forest Qigong moved into its first healing center, on the second floor of a small three-story office building. From then on, we saw many people each day for healing sessions.

People sometimes assume that it's a one-way process, that the magic is done by the healer. The healer supplies a certain amount of expertise, but the person receiving that healing energy knows about what they need. They may not know it consciously, but somewhere inside, they know about comfort. Somewhere inside, they know about peace. Somewhere inside, they know just as much as the healer what their need is. When you, as a healer, help them, you are letting them know, you are giving them a signal—that signal says: I am here to help. This is how I can help.

Teaching

As a young adult, I went to visit a career counselor, as was common then, to take a test and get an assessment on what kind of work I was suited for. I was eighteen years old and had recently discovered martial arts. I taught karate part-time and loved it. When I told this counselor that I was interested in pursuing a career in martial arts, they proceeded to inform me it was not possible—I would have no success and make no money. They advised me to go a different direction.

A couple of decades later (after becoming a career counselor myself), I was about to change my direction completely. I would quit working for the school district, where I was in line for an administrative position, so that I could dedicate all my time to Qigong. After meeting Master Lin and witnessing the effectiveness of Qigong practice and healing firsthand, I knew I wanted to make it my primary focus in life, and this was my chance. I would not let it pass by. It was 1998 when I quit my career with the public schools and began working full time at the Spring Forest Qigong Healing Center.

I continued to attend Master Lin's classes, offer healing work, and practice the movements and meditations each day. We traveled many places as Master Lin gave lectures and classes, sharing the knowledge of this ancient healing art. I witnessed people as they were filled with joy in receiving information about how they could help themselves to live a happier, healthier life, and the beautiful message that everyone was born a healer. The Spring Forest Qigong techniques were simple enough for everyone, no matter what age or ability, and the results were astounding. Students were seeing positive effects physically and mentally after just a few days of practicing.

One day, as Master Lin was in the middle of teaching a level one class, he paused and said, "Jim, you teach the rest of the class."

When he gathered his things and left the room, I was even more surprised. In that moment, there was so much trust and confidence coming from him as I walked to the front of the classroom. Though he had never witnessed me lead a class, he knew I had experience, and most importantly—he believed in me. In his own way, and from the heart, he let me know I was ready. I had been watching and listening to classes for several years—now it was my turn.

While teaching Qigong, sometimes I made mistake after mistake (my students can attest to this, I can hear them now)—I said the wrong words, or put them in the wrong order, or forgot my place completely. Everything became so ridiculous and funny in these moments; the class would explode into laughter. Master Lin witnessed this situation one day.

"This is really good," he said. "When people laugh, a great opportunity for healing is there. When they laugh and smile, they just open up."

I taught many classes from then on; great joy accompanied all of them.

We are more than what we think we are. You can change things in an instant. The effects are so profound, sometimes people have a hard time accepting it. Many times, healing and transformation are possible at a level which looks to be miraculous. I have had the honor to witness this over the years. Spring Forest Qigong, in my experience, can help people discover this for themselves.

In the beginning levels of Spring Forest Qigong classes, I taught students the power of their minds, their emotions and intention, and how these areas affect our health and healing. To demonstrate, I would ask a student to come up to the front of the classroom and invite them to sit in a chair. I'd ask them if they were feeling any discomfort anywhere. Perhaps they had a stiff neck, or the joints in their fingers were sore. Usually, there was something. Then, I asked another student to come forward. This student became the healer. I guided them briefly on how to help the healing energy flow within the first student's body, and then to remove any blockages—sending them back into the universe. After only a few minutes of the student-healer helping to send healing energy—the student seated, who had discomfort, either no longer felt it, or reported a noticeable improvement in the area. They consistently said that they felt better. After completing the process, both the student healer, and the student experiencing the healing, in a few short moments, went through a series of emotions—surprise, then hopefulness, and then a renewed confidence in themselves and their ability to get well.

After all the years I had spent teaching and working with kids, it was a surprising joy to be teaching adults Qigong and witness such a transformation. After experiencing healing firsthand, everyone in the class realized the implications: *If it is possible to change the body with our intent, with our thoughts, and in only a few moments' time, what else was possible? How much do our thoughts and emotions influence our bodies, our environment?* The paradigm had shifted. Everyone in the room discovered a new way of looking at their lives.

I can't help but think sometimes about all the people I worked with in the past—the kids on the street, school kids, community people—many of these people could have benefitted greatly from knowing Qigong. Many I've encountered felt like they did not have a place in life. They felt like they were not important, or had no talent, and no skills to offer. I sometimes imagine being able to go back in time and show them Qigong, telling them how beautiful, how powerful, and how worthy they are—and all without having to do a thing. We are born this way. This healing energy, this work, is so accessible to everyone.

Rainbows, Flowers, Sunshine

I was invited to teach kids Qigong through a community college program. It was a summer program for kids. Before the class began,

I received a letter in the mail. A young girl, age five, wrote it. The letter read: *Please, may I join your class? I am 5 years old. I promise I will be really good and work hard. My sister is in the class. I want to learn Qigong too.*

The class was officially for ages six to ten. But, of course, I said yes to her joining the class, even though she was a little younger. For a day, I taught the kids about how to do energy healing work using the Spring Forest Qigong techniques. Teaching kids Qigong is simply wonderful. They are wide open, filled with curiosity, excitement, and willingness—they embrace Qigong like they have been waiting for it all along. When it comes to kids and Qigong, there is no hesitation, no doubt—they understand the concepts quickly (often faster than adults) and are ready to go out into the world with their new skills and start helping people right away.

The little girl who wrote me the letter did well in the class. She was attentive and confident. With seriousness, she practiced the techniques I taught to clear blocked energy. After leaving class that evening with her older sister, she waited at home for her father to return from his workday. Usually, every day when he came home, he had a sore and stiff back. He went straight to the sofa to lie down for the rest of the night.

On this evening, though, his youngest daughter approached him as he came through the front door.

"Daddy! I can fix your back! Let me do Qigong for you... Please?"

Well, he thought there was no harm in letting her try out what she learned at school. So, she went to work, practicing everything she learned in Qigong class—breaking up the congested energy, and then removing any blockages and excess energy, sending it back into the universe as light.

After she finished, she asked her father to get up from the sofa and walk around the room.

"You feel better, right?" she asked with a smile.

He was already prepared to tell her what a good job she did and how he felt better—even if there was little difference. But to his great surprise, as he stood up and paced around the living room, he found no pain in his back. A puzzled look grew on his face.

He thought, *the pain is not there.*

Not only was it absent from his back, but the pain was gone from his knees and joints as well, which were usually stiff and sore. For the first time in fifteen years, the unrelenting back pain had disappeared. At home with his daughters that evening, he found himself almost speechless.

The next day, when I returned to school to teach another class with the kids, I found the father and his two girls waiting for me in the hallway. With tears shining in his eyes, he told me the story of how his youngest daughter healed his back. Weeks later, after the class was over, I received a package in the mail. It was full of crayon drawings—rainbows, flowers, sunshine—all from the five-year-old who made her case to take my Qigong class, and then went home to heal her father. I hung the bright drawings on the walls of my office at the Healing Center. I still smile when I think about them today.

You have to start looking at your life like it means something every single minute of the day. You don't want to lose opportunities. All of a sudden, this kind of thing starts rolling into your world.

Skills for Life

In the lifestyle of an athlete, an injury could change everything—in an instant. One minute, crowds of people could be cheering. I could feel the rush, the fans filling the air with excitement and encouragement. In another moment, though, I could be injured badly. I could find myself alone, crawling across the floor with no skills and no future.

The skills I gained through my work in helping children and adults would always be with me. They would always be useful. I recall the words of my father as he encouraged me to find a focus. He believed that if I had a trade, something with which I could help others, I would be alright in the world, my work would always be needed. The ability to work with healing, with teaching, and being of service to others, were skills that would carry me throughout my life, and continue to teach, and to heal me.

One day, a woman came into my office for healing. I cannot remember what her condition was, but it was quite serious and deeply rooted. As I sat with her, preparing to do what I could to help, something came to my mind that told me I needed to sing for her. Then, a melody came to me. I sang softly as she sat in the chair across from me. In that moment, I knew, great healing took place, and as I finished the song, I noticed gentle tears streaming down her face.

Another time, a friend came to see me. He had been diagnosed with cancer and was on his way to a well-known clinic for a second screening. As he sat in my office telling me his story, I saw out of the corner of my eye a flash of color, bright red, suddenly appeared in the window. There was a woman seated beside this man, and she pointed to a red bird perched on the windowsill. Right then, in that moment, I knew something had changed. Everything shifted, I could feel it—healing had taken place. Later that evening, my friend called me on his way back from the doctor's visit.

"There was nothing there!" He exclaimed. "Nothing! The doctor could hardly believe his eyes. It's gone!" The cancer was completely gone.

You never know what it could be that comes along with healing—a song, a color, an image—this extraordinary energy, this intelligent energy, I've learned, can be so playful; and it knows the situation much better than anyone else in the room. I have learned that trust and patience are some of the greatest gifts when working with healing at any level. It is good to remember that healing is already there. It is always within us and all around us.

During my time working at the Spring Forest Qigong Healing Center, I witnessed so many things that many would call miraculous, not only from the work I was doing, but I also saw miracles through others working at the center, and through students using techniques they had learned in classes. So many healing events happened every day, it is impossible to recall them all. It was so empowering—the presence of hope, the possibility of complete healing. Through these miracles and stories, it was very clear to me that some other force—one which was much greater and more intelligent than myself—was at work.

Sometimes the seriousness of the healing that needed to take place was so great, I simply did not know what to do. I would take a moment of stillness and call out for help. Each time, as I sat in that chair, and across from me sat another human being, who was there asking for my help, I'd say silently, *Ok God, you do it.* I always had it in my mind that I was not doing the work on my own. There was no way, without the help of an intelligence far greater, that these healing miracles were possible; and I was fortunate enough to see them. The divine always came through, and many times, in the most astounding ways.

Healing has its own intelligence. When you are working with people, you have to understand that this intelligence is helping you figure out and see what can work. Sometimes people think it's between two people, but sometimes it's more than that. It's between people and the land. Sometimes it's between people and their DNA. Sometimes it's between the environment that reaches out beyond the knowledge of this land.

Sometimes it's in the vibration in the sky, in the stars. Sometimes it's in the understanding of the will of the divine for this person that you find that information. As a healer, you get information that helps you.

The Fisherman

My friend was attacked by a shark one day while out fishing. He lived on a small island, quite a distance from where I was. Fishing is how he makes his living, how he supports his family. He contacted me and told me what he experienced. He was out spear fishing one day, and just after he had speared a fish, a shark appeared. The shark, smelling the blood of the fish he caught bit into his forearm and hand. Fortunately, he was able to get away. But he could no longer use his hand. His wrist did not bend, and his fingers had frozen into a twisted position—the skin along his hand and forearm tight and rigid. After hearing his story, and seeing a photo he sent me of his hand, with its scarred skin and damaged muscles—I thought, *how and am I going to work with this?*

Then, I waited in stillness—thoughts came to me about my friend. Information started streaming in rapidly:

He depended on the use of his body in the water to help him fish. He used his hands all the time. But he needed to understand the water. He needed to understand the electrical experience that went on in his body when he saw a fish—the experience that went on when he was about to catch a fish. He needed to know something about the intelligence of that entire process.

Learning comes into place. When I reached the place to work with him on an energetic level, I had to understand about who he was, what he does, and what his needs are in life. I saw the need to care for his children, the need to be of service to others. To care for and provide for his family, he needs to understand the water that he swims in. He needs to understand the sunlight that will help him clearly see the fish that know how to disguise themselves. He needs to have a wealth of knowledge. And without that, well, he can't do it.

So, what I did was ask the universe, ask God, for information about the science of fishing, and all that is involved for this friend. I asked for information to come forward about the body's intelligence—the intelligence that will help him better do, or continue to do, what he needs, to be functional, to continue his work. I received more and more information. Eventually, I understood the muscle structure of his arm. I understood the skin. I understood his motivation for wanting to be well. I started to understand all these things. To name them all is massive because there is a lot—but you find that as you are doing the healing, you will be educated along the way. As a healer, you are listening to your own processes, and your processes can lead to a healthy result, a successful result, and the ability to tap into the information that is needed.

The energy understands you; it understands your intent. It knows that if you have strong faith or belief, it can do anything. That is going to help you in the healing process. If you can instill this perspective into the person you're working with, at some level, if they can just get a peak, then sometimes it's enough to open the door. When the two of you are working toward the same end, it magnifies the energy that you're working with. It also strengthens the knowledge within that energy so that you get the result that's the most desired. So, you can take a hand that has been mangled by a shark and you can repair it, because the vision is there, and it is a shared vision. It starts at the seed, which is who that person is in the world, and who you are in the world.

I worked with my friend, the young fisher, for several weeks. After the first week, he began to be able to move his fingers and wrist slightly. The next week, there was a little more mobility and flexibility. After a few weeks, he sent me a note, it read:

"Today, for the first time in months, I was able to give my young son a bath."

A few weeks later, after he continued to strengthen his tendons and muscles, I received a photo. He was standing proudly in his fishing boat, a bright glow of light beamed all around him.

It's all about listening. And it's a lot about trust. And then it's a lot about hope, faith, and all those things that people talk about in religion. All those things people talk about in health, and in education. All those elements come together to help you be successful in the process of healing.

Intelligent Energy

When I had the opportunity to learn Qigong from Master Lin, after twenty-seven years of searching, it seemed as natural as sunlight. I walked into it with confidence; knowing that this was something I was supposed to do. In ways, it felt like Qigong came to me so easily—but on other levels, there were major struggles. But there was a complete pull. I was drawn into Qigong with my whole being. There is no limit to where you can go—as far as I've been able to see. What I'm learning about more and more is—how that limitlessness is linked to an intelligence. That intelligence is as real as the experience we have in life and our reason for being here. Our reason, our purpose for being here, goes far beyond what we can clearly see.

Why do we, at some point, have an urge for movement? Why do we, at some point, explore rest? Why do we think about things that we don't understand? There is so much knowledge that intuitively drives us in our lives. We lie down, and we go to sleep without the knowledge of sleep. We rest, and our body rejuvenates itself. There is no exercise, no meditation that we know of, no prayer to learn about sleep, about rejuvenation. But there is an intelligence that knows the body more than we intellectually understand. Our body understands what we need.

This intelligence affects everyone differently. The way it affects me through Qigong is that there are things I just know, things that I don't have to think about. When I am working as a healer, information comes to me, and I just know in an instant what I need to know. It moves me to work with people in unique ways. Like sleep, it is something that knows. The intelligence of Qigong is the same, and in deeper ways. The more you commit to it, the better you are at working with it.

It opens the door to you when you say: I'm willing to go through whatever door it is you need me to go through. So, if you need to understand something like color, for instance, and how color plays a significant role in your life, the intelligence will open itself up to you so that you have an opportunity to learn about color. You may have an opportunity to learn about health through color. Then, when you are ready to learn even more about the intelligence that is related to the color, you will get more insight, something that goes beyond anything you've ever been introduced to. Qigong knows you. This science is a science that understands you to the core. It awakens itself within you.

When I made the decision to devote my time to the study of Qigong, the intelligence of Qigong awakened within me. Previously, my life had no direction in this way. I didn't know that this type of healing science existed. As I continued to work with people, with Qigong, my understanding increased, and my desire to know more increased. When you have that desire to know, knowing comes to you. This knowing, then, opens the door for you to learn more. It is an automatic process.

Sleep comes to you so that you know about resting, so that you know about rejuvenating your body. Knowing comes to you for a similar reason. It comes to you to help you understand how to know, how to work with knowledge, how to work with the intelligence of knowing. If you want peace, and if you really want it, you will find out, at some point, that there is a doorway into the understanding of peace.

When we ask questions, the information comes. The information is always there to help. The difficulty we have is not in interfacing with this intelligence. The difficulty we have is understanding what it is we are listening to. The best way I have found is to educate myself into this process of learning, into the process of understanding. Sometimes, I may misunderstand. But when I misunderstand, this knowing lets me know I am not on the right track. I need to wait, and trust that the answer will come. Not putting the process on my timeline, but instead, placing my intelligence on its timeline—so that the intelligence will awaken, and the knowledge that I need to understand the dilemma, or the challenge, and the insight that I need, will come forward.

Sitting

Sitting in meditation was extremely painful at first, even while sitting still in a chair. When I went into a deep, meditative state of mind, pain would erupt all over my body. Damage ran deep into my system because of the injuries from high-impact sports, and as I let my body and mind slow down and enter a quiet state, the experiences that my physical body had gone through over the years, the reverberations of many jarring collisions, all came to the surface. It was as if I was finally allowing my body the space and the opportunity to express its grievances. The body-memory was just as painful, or even more so, than the physical sensation at the time of the injury. But I was determined to keep sitting and meditating. The intense pain slowly became softer, though, and gradually began to fade.

My body needed the time and the chance to regain a sense of self that would allow healing to take place at a complete level—an emotional level, as well as physical. Quietly sitting still and allowing the healing energy to go to work within me was just what I needed to do.

When I finally sat on the floor in a cross-legged position, the sensations were even more intense, but I kept at it. It was a slow process. I learned from my experiences as an athlete, if I kept going, little by little, day by day, moment by moment, I would one day reach my goal. It was important to me to gain the skill of sitting still and meditating for longer periods of time. I knew it would help strengthen my energy, and then I could help more people. My goal was to meditate in the full-lotus position.

ONE LEG CROSSES OVER THE OTHER

BOTTOM OF FOOT FACES UPWARD

FULL LOTUS

Eventually, the day came when my body felt ready. After getting my legs into the posture, at first, the sensation was so intense that tears streamed down my face. As I sat, I always had a box of tissues near at hand. Once again, little by little, I practiced sitting in the position, adding time incrementally.

When the time came for me to sit for two hours—an extraordinary shift took place. As I sat with my eyes closed, images appeared. Faces of people who I had never seen before appeared, their images flashing rapidly before my mind. All the people I saw in my vision, it was clear, were experiencing great pain and suffering. Hundreds, perhaps thousands of faces were streaming by in rapid succession as I sat—faces, expressions of people from many cultures, from all around the world, and from all throughout time. Even though my own physical discomfort was great, I could see that the pain these people experienced was much greater. Their images, along with their stories and struggles, kept passing before me without pause. The feeling of wanting to help them relieve their pain and suffering was overwhelming. The feeling of compassion was so strong it was almost unbearable. Faster and faster, the vision presented many people before me—thousands. And then, as abruptly as it began— it stopped.

In the silence, in the dark—there, staring directly at me, was a pair of eyes. They were all that I could see. They filled the whole screen of my vision. Filled with kindness, compassion, and love—I knew in an instant—*these eyes belong to the one they call Jesus.*

After that experience, I was able to sit for two hours every day. In the morning, before going to work, and again when I came home in the evening, I sat to meditate. I followed this routine daily, always at the same time of day, for several years. Until one day, when a friend approached me while at work and told me she had a dream. In that dream she was given a message: *Jim Nance needs to sit in meditation for five hours.* When I heard this, I felt like I would fall over. But I heard the truth in her words, and I knew that this was what I needed to do next.

The way I went about my practice was to find the way that was right for me. Master Lin taught me that everyone is unique in their practice, and it is important to find a way of practicing that feels right for you. One's purpose for practice—one's intent—is highly important, as this will have a direct influence on how things proceed. As I learned more, and grew in my practice, I kept these things in mind: always to have clarity about my purpose, and to follow the wisdom and the direction of my teacher.

I continued to sit in meditation for five hours in the morning before I went to work at the Healing Center; and then again, after I came home from work, I sat for another five hours. I found that, during this time, I only needed a few hours of sleep each night. My primary purpose for long sitting meditation was to become a better healer. I wanted to do the best I could to help the people who came to see me each day. I followed this schedule of meditation for five years.

You reach a point where you become the perspective you need in order to embrace the intelligence you need. From there, your perspective continues to grow. It is not something you can place into a category because it is everything around you, and it is everything within you. You are understanding all of this while you are living your life, having new experiences, understanding new ways to heal, new ways to help, new ways to exist. You move deeper and deeper into an intelligence that is constantly breathing life into everything you do, everything you are, everything you see.

An Intimate Understanding

A majestic ginkgo tree sat only a short ways from my childhood home in Iowa. I was fascinated by its leaves and could be found sitting on the ground near its trunk quietly examining a leaf or two.

At a certain age in my life, I wondered why I had been seeking and searching for intimacy in ways that I didn't identify as intimate. Like, spending time touching a ginkgo leaf—looking at the color, wondering why the leaves were very similar, but not the same. I smelled the leaf. I noticed that some leaves had straight lines going through them, and then on other leaves, there might be a shorter line, or a line that was a little crooked. I spent time, in my early years, looking to understand these subtler levels of intimacy.

At eight, I wanted to learn more about movement and my physical body. So, I ran for eight hours. I wasn't tired at the end of that run, but at the end of that eight hours, I understood something about myself that I didn't understand before. At the end, I couldn't feel my body. It was almost like I had run myself out of a connection to my body, or to the body that I had before. Yet it was also the opposite. I ran myself into a new understanding of myself within my body. It had something to do with completion. This too, was a level of intimacy.

This kind of search went on. When I hit adolescence, I wanted to be more in touch with intimacy again, but this time I wanted to have a relationship with a girl, to form a friendship. I didn't want to go to parties. I didn't want to go see movies; the things that kids my age usually did. I wanted to sit down on the porch, or sit in a field, or sit in the forest. I wanted to talk to find out what made this person who they were.

Well, eventually, I learned that the intimacy I thought I was seeking was actually educating me all along—on its importance, and on my need to know more about it. It was difficult to understand what I was looking for. It seemed that what everyone was showing me about being intimate was not right for me.

Around that time, in my adolescence, when I was most in need of understanding what intimacy was, I had the opportunity to be surrounded by nature—within the woods and in the fields, around plants and animals, colors, and new sensations. I began to understand that the meaning of intimacy went much further than what I had been shown. I saw it went beyond people.

I found I could learn about its meaning and value through other living beings—trees, insects, animals—and I learned in ways that didn't include spoken language. It was a language that went beyond words. What I discovered was that intimacy was a word that simply meant—close relationship, close communication—closeness at a divine, at a unifying degree, to the living world. And that door opened to a further understanding. It changed the way I saw the world. This process continues to this day—knowing who I am as a new being. It never stops.

When I first started practicing Qigong, I was not in a romantic relationship with anyone, nor did I have any interest. As I started doing more work with healing, it became clear to me that I had found something very serious—something which required my complete focus and time. Being in an intimate relationship, sharing my life closely with another, meant that my time would be divided. I knew I had to make a big decision—to dedicate myself fully to Qigong and healing work, or to pursue a relationship. A voice from within asked, *how long have you been waiting for this opportunity with Qigong?* To help many people, and to the degree that I wished to help them, I knew I could not be divided in my focus. As I was considering the implications of this, though, I continued to date casually.

One day, I was visiting a woman whom I was dating. It was around noon, and we were at her house. Suddenly, as I was sitting in the kitchen by myself, a giant figure appeared in the doorway. He was so huge, he could not fit through the door frame. He lingered outside, peering in at me. His head was as wide as a car. He had the physique of a bodybuilder, standing over eight feet tall, with arms like tree trunks. He was the biggest human I had ever seen. Though, I knew the truth—he was not human. He was the angel called Michael.

We stared at each other for a long moment. His expression stern and hard, told me he was not happy with me. I waited and kept still. Through my thoughts, he communicated to me. If I continued to do what I was doing, he told me—to date casually, I would come into great harm and end up in deep regret. If I kept on the way I was going, I would surely see him again (and the next time would not be for a cup of tea and a chat). After one more intimidating glare, he turned and disappeared. After he was gone, I walked out the front door of the house, looked both ways, and never came back. The message was loud enough for me. My mind was made clear. I knew I would dedicate at least part of my life to being alone. This began a period of celibacy that lasted eighteen years.

A clarity I received, only much later, was that I had yet to understand, or to experience, what intimacy truly was. Having an uncommitted attitude to such an important aspect of life would inevitably come to harm me. Even before a relationship began, I felt I could easily walk away at any time. This perspective, I came to understand, would hurt my healing ability; and it may damage my life on a spiritual level that may take lifetimes to undo.

Step by Step

Driving down the highway in Minnesota, I watched as the cars is front of me swerved back and forth between the lanes. My car started doing the same. The snow was falling so hard that the sky and the road became one unified, flat, white dimension. I decided it was best to get off the highway, and so I pulled over and phoned a friend. I knew she lived nearby. I asked to stop by their house and wait out the storm. She and her husband were watching a football game as the snow continued to fall in thick flakes. I joined them. Finally, after a couple of hours, the torrential weather eased up, and I left. On the way out, going down the stairs that led to the road, I suddenly slipped and fell. I heard a snapping sound in my knee and knew right away something was wrong. With one hand, I felt around for my knee. All I could feel at the joint were bones loosely moving around as if there was nothing holding them together— like sticks in a sack. I was so accustomed to pain, though, that the discomfort did not feel completely unbearable. Somehow, I got up and continued the walk to my car.

The next day, I saw Master Lin.

When he looked at my knee, he said, "This is serious, Jim. Most likely you are going to need surgery."

"I really don't want surgery," I protested. "I think I can heal it. I want to try."

"Well, in order for this to heal completely, you are going to need to convince an angel to come down from heaven." He replied.

"Then I would like to call on that angel for two weeks and see if we can heal it." I said.

"Two weeks is too long," he cautioned.

I went back home, determined to try my hardest to heal myself. I had several surgeries in my life already and did not want to be cut open again.

Then, about a week later, on another snowy Minnesota evening, I was coming out of a hardware store, crossing the parking lot, when I slipped on a patch of what Minnesotans call black-ice. The ground appears solid and stable, and looks like pavement, but it's not. This time, after I fell, I heard and felt the terrible snap in the other knee. My leg twisted as I hit the ground, so that after I fell, it was bent in the opposite direction. Instead of the leg bending backward at the knee, my leg folded forward. At this point, I knew that it was not likely I could avoid surgery. An ambulance was called, and I was taken the hospital.

The amazing thing was—the healing energy began its work right away on my knee. I could feel the qi at work. By the time I was able to see a doctor, I could stand and move around. From an outside perspective, everything appeared to be normal. I was walking, talking, and did not exhibit any pain symptoms. When the doctor asked what the concern was, I told him the story of both falls, and both knees. After he examined them, he looked me in the eye.

"This is very serious," he said. "You're going to need surgery."

"But I can move around, no problem." I protested, "Check this out."

And then I proceeded (to the doctor's shock and horror) to squat almost all the way to the ground.

"That is incredible," he said, unnerved, "but you really shouldn't do that. You might cause more damage."

In both knees, the ACL tore completely. This is the part of the knee that stretches down from the thigh muscle, extending over the kneecap, and attaching to connecting ligaments in the lower part of the leg. Like a big elastic band, with tension, it holds all the bones of the knee in place as they meet at the joint. Without it, the bones would not hold together, and the legs could not hold the body upright.

This injury is common within the world if sports, and full recovery, I knew, was rare. Fortunately, some of the best surgeons in the field were in Minnesota at that time. They had been working with athletes from the Minnesota state football team. Before they began the operation on my knees, I insisted that Master Lin be present in the room, and graciously, the doctors allowed it. For over six hours they worked without rest, to reattach, layer by layer, all the tendons and muscles in both knees. Master Lin told me later, that as he watched, he saw beams of light shooting out from the inside of my body.

The hospital prescribed heavy doses of pain medication following the surgery, but stubbornly, I refused them as they released me from the hospital. I thought I could handle the pain. Later, though, as I lay in bed at home, I spoke with Master Lin on the phone and told him I didn't accept the pain medication. Telling me how difficult the surgical procedure was, he reminded me how long it took, and what excellent work the surgeons did on my legs.

"If you don't take the medicine," he said, "you could have a muscle spasm in the night and tear through all the hard work they did."

After hearing this, I called the hospital. They had to come back to pick me up, and I took the medication they prescribed.

The whole time through recovery, also before and after the accident, I called on help from the divine. As I lay in bed, unable to move, I constantly prayed. Soon, with the help of crutches and braces that held my legs stiffly in place, I started inching around my house in short lengths of time. But my legs could not bend while in the braces, and I became worried, not that they wouldn't heal, but that they might heal so fast that I would lose flexibility in the joints permanently. They had been bound up for so long. I was eager to get back into sitting meditation practice, but I had to be patient.

Soon, though, the braces came off. So, with great care, I began to bend my knees little by little. Seated in a chair, I practiced bending one knee the slightest bit, almost an unnoticeable amount of movement, and then I held it there for a moment. Tending to both knees, I repeated this gentle bending movement at least three times each day. I began, slowly, in small increments, to bend them further. Until, one day, I could pick up my foot while seated in a chair, and place it onto my lap, with my knee bent out to the side. When I saw I could achieve this level of flexibility, I had confidence I could go further.

Eventually, after a slow, careful, and gradual effort, I was sitting in a half-lotus position (cross-legged in a seated position with just one foot set on the opposite thigh). And not long after that, full lotus. I knew that what had happened to my knees was serious, and to fully recover, I needed to continue to be serious about doing all I could to heal. Slowly working my way into longer and longer sitting meditation, soon I was sitting for 10 hours straight each day. I had a couple of months off from work at the Healing Center, so I sat in deep meditation every day, strengthening my legs, as well as my spiritual and healing energy. During this period, I experienced my first enlightenment.

When I went to see my doctor, he asked how my flexibility was so far.

"It's going really well," I replied.

The doctor took my leg carefully in his hands and tried bending it at the knee, then he bent it a little more, and then some more. I saw his eyes grow wide as he bent it all the way. He wasn't expecting much flexibility.

"I want to show you something," I said.

Then, sitting on the floor, I pulled one foot across to rest on my thigh, and then the other. I am sure the doctor had not seen many people in the full lotus position—and certainly not someone who recently went through double ACL surgery. He was nearly in shock. He stood staring for a moment, his mouth slightly ajar.

"This is impossible!" he exclaimed.

It had been only three weeks since I had the surgery.

A greater challenge than sitting or gaining flexibility was relearning how to walk. An idea came to me one day while watching a movie. In the movie, I noticed there were many scenes, often they were scenes depicting the place or setting, including images of people walking. It might be a downtown business crowd, or people walking through the mall, or a park. So, I rented a stack of movies and spent hours examining the actors' movements, studying how they walked. Sometimes I paused the scene to look more closely at the body position, or some specific area, like the leg muscle, or foot placement.

Then one day, during meditation, I had a vision: My view was through a narrow portal. Positioned in a way so that my eyes were at ground-level, I saw a street, and people walking by. I only saw the bottom portion of people—their hips, legs, and down to their feet. I could view a whole crowd as they walked directly in front of me. It was like looking out of a basement apartment window at street level.

Through this vision in my meditation, I could study anatomy and movement even more clearly than through the movies. I learned more about the active process of walking, regarding each muscle as they engaged to move each leg in the right way. After this experience, I was able, slowly, to walk again.

The events that happened with my knees, and then with my recovery, were exceedingly rare, the doctors informed me. First, that the supportive ligaments (ACL) in both knees were severed at around the same period of time was something they didn't see often. Usually, in sports, or other accidents, only one knee is damaged, but not both at the same time. The second uncommon thing was the degree of damage to the tissue. The ligaments on both knees were completely torn. One knee was a little worse than the other, but both were damaged at a very high level. The doctors did not expect me to have a full recovery. And then, not only did I recover, and could walk again, but my flexibility was much greater than the average person—and all in under three weeks' time.

I credit this extraordinary degree of healing to Qigong, the skills I learned from Master Lin, and of course—all the prayers, and the ongoing support of the divine.

Qigong Master

Witnessing the tireless efforts of Master Chunyi Lin and his ability to call on support to help him do the things he needs to do—not from people, but from the universe, from the divine—I have been able to see this intelligence at work. How it has supplied him with the information, the people, the materials, and the success he has needed to move on to the next step. I have witnessed how he has accepted all of that support with such an attitude of graciousness, with such an attitude of respect and honor, and love. I see how that support energizes him to be even more tireless in his effort to serve others. It is the closest that I have ever found in my life to witnessing a person functioning on a high spiritual level.

This divine presence not only works through him as he works with people, but it also works through the environment as he is working with people. It is like he is a magnet for service—and the universe sends him what he needs to do the things that he does. It's ongoing. It's never ending. I have yet to see it stop. What I've learned about being of service in this world, I have had the great fortune to witness the actualization of, through my friend and teacher, Master Chunyi Lin.

To go from a place where I felt that my knowledge of Qigong was limited, to one day, the question that Master Lin proposed—*would I like to be a Qigong Master?* It is hard to put into words how massive the idea was to me.

I was so in awe of Master Lin. I never had a desire for people to see me in the light of a Master—perhaps someday I may be a high-level student, I thought, but I never imagined that I could be a Qigong Master. After spending time around Master Lin, I saw he was a student of life. It is hard not to be in a state of awe around someone like that—one who not only studies things from a day-to-day perspective, but one who understands things that go so far back, through layers of time, through history.

I was not yet aware of all the skills I possessed. I didn't understand all the things I had going for me, or the potential. But based on what I saw in Master Lin as a human being, I trusted that if he believed I could be a Qigong Master, then I was willing to say—yes, I'll do it. After going through those thoughts, I began to recall the successes I had as a healer during the time I worked with Qigong. I looked at all the things that happened that were miracles to me—things that sometimes I felt overwhelmed by.

I could not deny the wonderful experiences I had with people I worked with. I received so much gratitude—I could never forget that. If what I was doing, I was doing at a master's level—then I wanted to continue doing it. It was so great to be of service in this way. Not all the counseling work that I had done, not the community work, even though I had many successes in the past, nothing compared in quite the same way to what I was experiencing with being of service through Qigong and healing.

After I accepted the designation (2004)—to be the first Spring Forest Qigong Master—I took many things into consideration. I knew that what I needed to do was create a complete focus with Qigong. It affected every aspect, every perspective of my life. Spring Forest Qigong would become the lens through which I saw the world and my life. Not a sports perspective, not an academic perspective—these things I already was acquainted with. I knew I would dedicate myself to the process of being a Qigong Master.

More and more, you move into a day-to-day practice— not where you are thinking about becoming anything, but where you just do what you can to develop a relationship between the movements you are making and the intelligence that you are trying to cultivate. There will be times when you experience things in a, let's say, a graduated level. But for the most part, it takes time. It takes work. You have to take it day by day— not one philosophical outcome to the next philosophical outcome.

Take a look at who you are in your practice from the perspective of how you move your hands, how you slow down your movements, how you handle controversy, how you handle places and challenges in your life. You start looking at your life like it is part of something that has been beautiful all along—innocence, language, land, weather, future. You begin to realize just how important healing is, not just from a physical level, but a historical level, a psychological level, and a physiological level as well.

Healing perspective, valuing perspective, choosing health, choosing wisdom, and not choosing oppression, not choosing ignorance—when those things come around in any form, you recognize, as a Qigong Master, that there are solutions.

There is a way of healing that can exist for all. There are people that are out there, waiting and wanting to be healed and to be supported.

Even though you cannot always reach everyone, you can reach somebody, and do little things at a time. Before you know it, a few grains of sand turn into an island. An island grows into a land mass—one that can be walked on, one that can be lived on—a whole world.

Being a Qigong Master, I wish I could go back fifteen thousand years and say to Lao Tzu: Thank you for coming up with this. Thank you for asking God to give you the wisdom to offer something to the world that is as massively beautiful as this.

The Visit

And then one day, after twenty-some years of practicing, you say to yourself—Goodness! I wish I could see Lao Tzu someday. I wish I could see how he looked. I don't know if I'll ever have that experience. And when you are ready to give in, you say: Okay, I have to accept what I can do. I have to accept what I can't do.

And then you go into a meditation:

You find you are surrounded by darkness.

All of a sudden, you see a light that is the size of the point of a needle.

That light begins to grow and grow.

The light is coming towards you, and the closer the light moves to you,

the more you see a form within that light, held by that light.

You look at it.

You look at it because you know there is a seed of knowledge in that light.

You are waiting for that seed of information to come through.

Because the seed may be helpful for you in the future.

The light just keeps coming.

And then, you see clearly that there is a face.

It's trying to force its way through the darkness.

All the while, this light is getting bigger and bigger.

And the face continues trying to poke its head through the darkness.

The face finally comes through.

Next, he pulls his body through that darkness.

You watch, and you wait.

And then the image of a person is standing there.

It is like all the images that you have seen of Lao Tzu,

And he is standing right in front of your eyes.

How can I possibly begin to say thank you to all of it for leading me to this place where I am sitting now—while looking at the image of this being who has stepped through all time, who has stepped through all these thousands of years, wishing for something within my lifetime? Who am I—having had the experience of something that was called up from some fifteen thousand years ago to be present in my meditation?

I waited, and we looked at each other in silence. And then the image of Lao Tzu moved back through the wonder, the darkness that he came through to see me.

And you realize, this is precisely the way the whole practice of Qigong has come to you in your life—not only when you find Lao Tzu standing there in front of you—but since the time you first realized you were a human being on this planet.

And it comes, not necessarily through the intelligence of knowing *here I am*, but from the intelligence of experiencing—Who am I? What's life? What's love? What's expertise? What's knowing? What's mastery? What's gratitude?

The darkness is simply a call. The misunderstandings are simply a call. The wonderings, all of it—a call to something so magnificent that you start to realize just how significant you are.

When you do this work, you don't lose ground. You don't lose ground when you commit to understanding your life and who you are, and what it means to be alive and searching—searching for understanding, searching for opportunities to serve.

If you don't know what peace is today—if you don't know what happiness, joy, contentment, gratitude is—trust that all you don't know is nothing compared to what knows you. If you can do that, then you can become something that is much more. You are bringing much more than you think into this work because the work is taking in you.

Qigong From the Heart

I feel that my whole life prepared me to open the door to Qigong. I had no idea what it was. How could I know that something as wonderful and as incredible as the Qigong that I have experienced was waiting for me?

I have learned so much about compassion. I have learned so much about consistency. I have learned so much about the beauty of life, the wonder of living, the care that goes into giving oneself to something. Qigong has helped me to understand more about service. More about being there, as a vehicle to support, not just people, but life of all kinds.

There is a vibration that you carry into your life, and that vibration affects everything. You don't have to do anything for this for this to happen. It is so important to gain clarity on who you are and why you are here. We are here, not just because we are here. We are here because there is a plan. We are doing what we are doing in Qigong daily, not just to do something good, but for the reason of building something wonderful— building a world that understands there is an intelligence on which to place yourself, the well wishes of others, the hopes that people have for their lives, for their children, for the land, for their environment. Qigong is a practice that helps you see beauty. Qigong helps you see life from the perspective of wonder. It embraces the magnificence of an intelligence that cares about the issues connected to living—to success, to health, to birth, to relationships filled with love, to futures, to a better world, to a better life.

The more you seek to understand that intelligence, the more you are in awe of how magnificent it is, and the more in awe you are of all the people through history who have worked hard, and consistently, to help make Qigong what it is—as special as it is. This is a science that is designed to meet the need for the betterment of the human condition.

The science of Qigong is always doing something to improve upon itself—it becomes better and better, as a practice, as a way of life. It grows, and it grows. And there are people out there working every day to increase that knowledge base. This I have learned from Master Lin, as I have watched him through the years, move into a mastery that goes far beyond things that one could even imagine. And he is standing on shoulders of all the people—the teachers, and the Masters that went before in studying this science.

Qigong acts, in its existence, to be of service, and can be a roadmap to people when they are asking questions like: How should I live? What is my life's meaning? How can I fix this issue that I've been dealing with forever? How can I learn to love? How can I learn to give something wonderful of myself to the world in which I live? How can I deal compassionately with people that are suffering around me?

All of this gives me great hope. Because I know there will be people in the future who will open their hearts. This practice makes way for newness to come in. It makes a place. It does not discourage. I am so glad that I searched as long as I searched for Qigong. This practice has made me a better human being.

Dear Friends,

How fortunate I feel to have had the life that I have. And where that would go in the book? Maybe at the end, maybe at the very end.

When you start to review all the things that you've done, and when you want to take an accurate assessment of those things, you tend to look at the world through a certain set of lenses. You realize, especially if you feel good about your life, that you are fortunate— to be wearing the lenses that you are wearing. You can rest on something beautiful, those beautiful memories propping you up. The possibility of beauty coming toward you becomes a stabilizing force, propelling you into the future.

When I look back, I realize I have learned so much more than I thought I did. The divine took so many beautiful opportunities to offer something wonderful to me in my life. And to think—I am where I am, doing what I'm doing. Goodness! I don't know how I could want for more than the support that I'm getting from the divine—to stand and walk, to laugh and love, and eat—and still be able to be of service to people. Every day, I get a chance to do something good for somebody. It is a very humbling thing—to be able to offer that, and to think about the all the people that help make it possible.

When I look at my future, I cannot deny that I've had wonderful people in my life to support me. And because this book is a book about my experiences in life, and becoming a Qigong Master, I couldn't have chosen a better person to study with. The environment that Master Chunyi Lin created was and is phenomenal. All the smiles, the support, all the gratitude, all the success. So much success! And all the people and magic involved through the decades—all of it came together in my life to form a path that would lead me to become the healer and person I am today.

Thank you for sharing in these stories.

Wishing you all the love your hearts can hold,

Master Jim Nance

After-words

In 2014, nineteen years after I first began to work with Qigong healing and teaching, I retired from Spring Forest Qigong. One year later, searching for a writer and illustrator for my picture book, *Jim and The Ants*, I found my wife, Naomi. I saw her wearing rubber boots, carrying buckets of water, tending to a batch of ducks and the vegetable garden in her yard (and she had the same name as my grandmother). I knew she was the one. My father's face appeared, smiling in the distance.

"If you ever find a horsewoman," he would say, "that's the kind you should marry."

Naomi and I married. Currently (upon completion of this book), we reside in Yucatan, Mexico, with our two border collies. We write books together, and I continue to offer healing services and give monthly lectures. Spiritual growth, healing, and deeper connection with the divine are lifelong pursuits. The learning never stops. I continue to grow and to cultivate my relationship with God each moment, finding new ways to be of service.

Resources:

Spring Forest Qigong: classes, practice groups, materials, and healing services. www.springforestqigong.com

Guiding Qi with Master Jim Nance: healing services, lectures, books, recordings. www.guidingqi.com

Naomi Joy Nance: art and writing, www.naomijoynance.com

Other books/ recommended reading:

Born a Healer, Master Chunyi Lin

Head to Toe Healing, Master Chunyi Lin

The Biology of Belief, Bruce Lipton

Zen Mind Beginner's Mind, Sunryu Suzuki

The Hidden Messages in Water, Masaru Emoto

The Wandering Taoist, Deng Ming-Dao

Tao Te Ching, Lao Tzu

Jim and The Ants: A True Tale, As Told by Master Jim Nance, N.J. Nance

Life and Teaching of the Masters of the Far East, Baird T. Spalding

The Bible

Master Jim Nance is a Spring Forest Qigong Master, a professional medical Qigong healer, teacher, speaker, and mentor. He received his bachelor's degree in education from Antioch College, and his master's in educational counseling from North Carolina Central, and taught in Minneapolis Schools for almost two decades. After twenty-seven years of searching for a Qigong Master, he met Chunyi Lin, an extraordinary Master from China. In 1995, he began learning Qigong through Master Lin. Soon after. Spring Forest Qigong was born (founded and created by Master Lin). After practicing and studying, Jim became a healer and instructor at the Spring Forest Qigong Healing Center in Minnesota and was named as the first Spring Forest Qigong Master in 2004. He continued to work as a healer at the SFQ Healing center until 2014 when he retired. Day to day, Master Jim Nance works to cultivate his Qigong practice and refine his healing technique while continuing to work to bring healing energy to people all around the world. He can be contacted for healing services, as well as written and audio materials through his website www.guidingqi.com

Naomi Joy Nance is the writer who worked alongside Master Jim Nance to turn his stories into words and get this book out into the world. She is a multidisciplinary artist, and has worked professionally in the areas of theater, dance, music, visual arts, and design. She is also the author/ illustrator of *Jim and the Ants,* a picture book created in collaboration with Master Jim Nance. Her visual art has seen audience in various venues around the United States, and she continues to create books, paintings, poetry, as well as to study and practice (daily) the ancient healing art of Qigong. Her website is www.naomijoynance.com